The Swagman & the Parson

Also by Jen Gibson and published by Ginninderra Press
Made in India

Jen Gibson & Russell Gibson

The Swagman & the Parson

The Swagman & the Parson
ISBN 978 1 76041 252 4
Copyright © Jen Gibson 2016
Cover photo: New South Wales Government Printer c.1901,
sourced from Wikimedia Commons

First published 2016 by
GINNINDERRA PRESS
PO Box 3461 Port Adelaide 5015
www.ginninderrapress.com.au

Contents

Foreword 7

The Swagman 9

The Parson 69

Postscript 144

Appendix: R.F. Gibson's Methodist Church circuits 146

Acknowledgements 147

R.F. Gibson

Foreword

This book contains two complementary stories written by two generations of the one family. It spans three centuries – from the 1860s to the present day, 2016. The swagman, Sully, and Russ Gibson, parson, were both born in the nineteenth century, though several decades apart. New South Wales was then a colonial state of Great Britain.

The story begins well before the federation of states into a Commonwealth of Australia. In the 1870s there were various great ships moored in Sydney Harbour to raise boys with no other means of support. They sound like the nineteenth-century poor houses described in Dickens's novels. Sully was one such lad who had begun life in an inner-city slum.

The tale of the swagman was penned in the 1970s by R.F. Gibson. I will leave my father to tell you that story in his own words with his early twentieth century turns of phrase and respect for language. At that time, a typescript was caringly prepared and checked from his handwritten original by my elder sister Raye Gibson. Very little has been altered for publication here, apart from a few typos. In one case, a possible confusion between a Border Leicester (a sheep) and a Border collie (a dog) was adjusted with a big smile. Distances are given in miles, the measurement of those days. References to pounds, shillings and pence (Australia's currency at the time) have also been left unchanged.

As children, my eldest sister Beryl, my sister Raye and brother Ken Gibson all knew Sully well. A child of my parents' older age, I was not born when the events of the swagman's tale unfolded. Nor was I familiar with south and western New South Wales, where many of the incidents took place. Once I knew that Ginninderra Press had accepted the story, I wanted to visit the inland NSW country places it describes and see them for myself.

The second half of the book, The Parson, is partly a narrative of that journey. It also incorporates my parents' oral memories recorded on tape in the early 1980s. These tapes have been transcribed after lying untouched for over thirty years. It was a peculiar experience listening to my parents' long-gone voices but it came to be a very enriching one. Having left it so long, it's now too late for me to clarify many things. Record your older family memories (or your own) in some verbal form if you can, dear reader. Ask some questions, sit back and let them talk. It's fun and often surprising. Do it now. It is often too late when we finally take an interest in our early heritage and family details.

I have incorporated parts of my parents' tape-recorded memories. They too are part of my journey back into the past. My mother was a friendly person. Her memories contain social details and are chatty. My father was by nature more philosophical and reflective. He used words sparingly and analytically. His tapes were made only one year before his death, when his memory was failing to some extent.

There is an old journal of my father's, a small leather-bound notebook, begun in 1909 when he was thirteen. At times I have quoted things he wrote there.

Various old photos of the Gibsons and the places they lived and worked have been included in this story – there were plenty to chose from. There are also some photos I took recently of the same locations. However, there is only one photograph of Sully the Swagman. You see him on page 68 – an old man in his newly acquired 'respectable' suit, with his dog. His beginnings (and what strange ones they were), you will have to imagine as you read on.

Jen Gibson

The Swagman

1

He was a little man, only five feet one inch in height. He was wearing tattered trousers, a tattered coat and a nearly respectable dark grey flannel shirt. There were several holes in his felt hat, through which hair protruded. Tousled hair hung down over the neck band of his coat, while a straggly greying beard grew over his whole face and came down to his chest. He carried a large swag, neatly folded. Tied to it were two dirty-looking black billies, one large and one small.

The midsummer morning was hot, and the road from Coolamon to Ganmain was flat and dusty – indeed, it was typical of the roads in the Riverina in the 1920s, bare of metal and often not even formed, with up to six inches of the finest dust in summer and a foot of sticky or slippery mud in the winter, with an occasional spot which the motor car wheels could not bottom and which sometimes bogged even horse-drawn vehicles.

As I steadied the car, a cloud of dust enveloped us both. 'Like a lift, mate?' I shouted.

He hesitated, looked at me and, as the dust cleared, came closer and said, 'Yes, if you're not a fast driver.' He hesitated again, then continued, 'A chap gave me a lift a few months ago and he went so fast and almost hit so many trees that I never expected to get out alive. Walking's pretty hard and the soles are worn off my boots, but I'd sooner walk than have that sort of ride. I get there, and I'm just as likely to get a job here as anywhere else.'

During these words, he came nearer and was looking closely at me. I knew from his expression that the decision was made and that he was accepting the lift.

Then I noticed something move in the larger billy. 'What's in the can?' I asked.

'Oh, that's a pup three weeks old,' he replied. 'I have to carry him from place to place so that the old lady can come too. She's followed me for eight years now, and when I have food she shares it. I can't have a lift unless you take her too.'

'Hop in,' I replied. 'I must get going.'

Leisurely and a little reluctantly, he threw his swag into the back of the car and, carefully adjusting the billies, he clambered over the swag on to the back seat. The black and white bitch, a border collie sheepdog noted for loyalty to one master, was already in and now sat proudly on the seat beside him, but she often glanced quickly at the larger billy to see that her offspring was safe.

There was now an odour of stale clothes in the car, which seemed to come equally from the swag and the man, while the aroma of the dog was not so distinct. The tramp clung tightly to the car, and through the rear-vision mirror I could see that he was not at ease.

With only a few sentences of conversation between bumps, concerning the weather, the dust and the flies, we arrived in fifteen minutes at Ganmain.

'I'll get out here,' he said, and there was relief and finality in his voice. Then, as he unloaded the swag carefully, because of the small tenant in the billy (the sheep dog had pushed out before him when she observed his intention), he asked, 'Can you direct me to the showground? I'll camp there and see some of the farmers tomorrow.'

I had a hunch food was short and said, 'How are you off for a bit of tucker?'

He answered evasively, 'I've got a bit of bread, I'll be all right.'

Sensing the position was worse than he admitted, I pressed two shillings into his hand. It was taken with reluctance and a look of gratitude. His only words were as convincing as they were unusual, and caused me to look at him closely.

'I don't drink, so the pub won't get it.' Almost inaudibly he mumbled something else which could have been 'thank you', as he adeptly adjusted the swag on his back and turned away.

I drove on, and before long had talked to many people about many things, and the little old swagman was out of my mind and likely to remain so.

2

It was not to end that way. Several years later, I met him again in a town several hundred miles away. Then I came to know him well, to learn of his life, his battle against overwhelming odds, his boyhood, his jobs and wanderings, his success and failure, his great shyness, his honesty, his determination, and the self-respect and dignity he preserved through all the years. Whether the odds against him were too great, whether his success was greater than his failure, I leave you, the reader, to decide.

This life story is closely wrapped with the child labour laws of New South Wales in the late nineteenth and early twentieth centuries. We go back to his childhood in the 1870s, and our story has its beginning in the largest city of Australia, the important and growing city of Sydney. Sydney already sprawling around a deep and beautiful harbour, with winding streets following the tracks of earlier days, conscious now of its greatness but not yet conscious of growing pains. Sydney with its noisy trams travelling with many jolts towards their destination and within vicinity of yours, with its hansom cabs plying to and fro to the crack of whips and the click clack of the steel-shod horses' feet on the wooden blocks with which the important streets were paved. Horse-drawn carts and wagons were going to and fro, and the beauty of the sleek well-groomed horses belonging to the breweries and to many large firms caused one to stop and look with admiration.

Nearby, in the suburb of Redfern, small houses, some stone, some brick, some of wood, had been built very closely together, chiefly for investment, by people living in England. Superior two-storeyed terraced houses were yet new and expressive of comfort. In one of the smaller wooden houses, with only a fifteen-foot frontage, lived a family by the name of Sully. There was only one child, a boy of about nine years. The house was built on the street alignment, and a broken window and lack of paint gave it a dilapidated appearance.

The father drove a team of horses carrying goods from the railhead and from the wharves to the stores. Occasionally he took the little boy, and the lad was proud indeed when he was permitted to hold the reins.

The father drank heavily, and frequently came home without money at the weekend. The boy dreaded weekends, not only because he was sometimes hungry, but because there were many quarrels and he was often flogged or kicked by a drunken and miserable parent.

The mother had long since lost heart for her work, although she did try to keep the home tidy and to grow a few things in the small backyard. But she had been worn down by lack of both money and cooperation. She tried to give her boy sufficient to eat, but often there was nothing in the home to cook and no money to purchase food, and she was dependent on the grocer who kept the small shop further up the street. The shopkeeper was kindly but because profits were small and business dull he could not help her as much as he wished. So the months and years passed by with little relief from fear of want, and no likelihood of better days.

Indeed, with the passing of time, less and less money came to the home, because the father used more and more of his earnings for drink. Floggings for the boy, nearly ten years of age, were at least weekly, and sometimes, in sheltering her son, the mother was abused and knocked down. With the driver seldom sober, and even in sober moments unhappy in himself and irritable with others, she began to fear for an accident with the horses.

It was a great shock but no surprise when one morning word came that Mr Sully had fallen from his lorry and was in hospital. The accident was caused by some harness breaking and while the driver was leaning on the rump of a horse, he slipped and fell to the ground among the horses' feet. The startled horses jumped forward and although he called them to stop, the thoroughly frightened animals moved enough for the wheels of the heavily laden wagon to crush his chest. He was taken unconscious to Sydney hospital. When his wife arrived, he was alive but scarcely conscious and sinking fast. She never forgot the look of fear on his face. He lapsed into unconsciousness and died that night.

The state bore the expense of burial. When other debts were paid, she had the sum of twenty-five shillings with which to pay rent and support herself and her little lad. The boy needed kindness to regain confidence and to develop initiative. Unwarranted thrashings, constant abuse and continued want had already arrested the development of this naturally shy lad. His world was insecure and he was full of fears.

What could his mother do? Constant work was not available. Wages for the work offering were insufficient to make ends meet, and there was no government pension to hold the home together. For a while, she tried hard, but the washing barely paid for rent and food, and there was nothing left for extras or for clothes. Soon the position became hopeless; she could not maintain her boy, and would have to hand him over as a ward of the state. The state would take him and find his food and clothing, and later employment. A friend told her that she would not be allowed to see him often, and although she had heard tales of hard-hearted employers, perhaps they were exaggerated and at least he would have sufficient food and clothing, and be given some education, which was more than she could do for him. God would guard her boy, and she had taught him to say a prayer at night too. She asked him not to forget that prayer, and she shed many tears when he left.

The police officer called at the bare home and gruffly but kindly took charge of the little chap. Tears trickled down the boy's cheeks as he turned from home and mother, but little did either of them understand the full meaning of this farewell. She accepted it as respite in the unequal struggle of life, and he accepted it as he had accepted the unwarranted floggings in his short hard life, with resignation. Indeed, he thought of it as the common lot of all young boys who had lost their fathers.

3

He was taken by the police officer to the *Sabraon*. The *Sabraon* was built in Aberdeen and launched in 1866 for the Australian trade. She was an almost perfect ship, containing a very large hold for cargo, and spacious passenger accommodation. Her tonnage was 2,131, with a length of 317 feet, and a beam of 40 feet, with a hold 40 feet deep. After many years with the Australian trade, the *Sabraon* was sold to the New South Wales government for £12,500 ($25,000). She was then refitted, moored in Darling Harbour and used as a government training ship for teaching and corrective purposes for boys receiving state help. It was regarded at the time 'as a successful place of correction and betterment for youth with a handicap in life'. These boys were afterwards known as State Boys. This ship replaced the old *Vernon* first used in the work, which was inaugurated in 1867. Still later, the *Sabraon* was refitted and used as an ark of naval learning for the young Australian Blue Jacket.

At the time of our story, the *Sabraon* was governed by a commander superintendent who was directly responsible to the government, and who submitted a full annual report to parliament. Here are extracts from a fine report by Commander Frederick Neitenstein, about this period. He writes,

> the year has been one of smooth working…the boys behaved well…no attempts to abscond…cheerful…contented…willing. Offenders were principally newcomers, and lads who came to us having proved incorrigible in other institutions. Numbers have been greatly increased… enrolment 451, the highest since inauguration in 1867. Health has been satisfactory. For the most part the boys come direct to us from some of the dirtiest parts of the city, where they have been in constant association with some of the most abandoned vagrants and thieves. Many arrive on board suffering from itch

and other skin diseases, vermin sores, want of proper food and neglect. No deaths have occurred. In 27 years there have been only 11 deaths in the institution or in hospital out of over 3,000 committed to us. Our class system is very effective and works on the principle of privileges and incentives. Although every boy committed is under the control of the institution until he is 18 years of age, he doesn't necessarily remain on the ship the whole of that time'.

No officer was permitted to strike any of the lads without authority. A chief schoolmaster prepared a timetable, and there was no school on Saturdays. Religious instruction was given by arrangement with the clergyman, or the lads were landed on Sunday and marched to their respective churches. There were also regular prayers at 9 a.m. and 9 p.m. which all had to attend.

Punishment was given by reduction in class, mastheading, confinement to punishment rooms and cells and corporal punishment with a cane. When six strokes or more were inflicted, the offence and the amount of punishment had to be recorded in the punishment book.

Visiting at the *Sabraon* was allowed as follows:

Parents, brothers, and sisters only of boys who have been over two months aboard will be permitted to visit the lads twice yearly...unless there are special reasons rendering such visits undesirable.

Visiting hours were between 1 p.m. and 3.30 p.m. on the first Thursday of January and July, and nothing was to be brought on board or given to the boys without the consent of the superintendent.

Such was the background for the training of Alfred James Sully, a lonely, diminutive, shy, frightened and backward boy. He thought of this floating training home as a prison. The officers and the discipline frightened him, but he tried hard to be obedient. He was not naturally disobedient, but he was backward and needed help that was not available on this ship of correction, and at the end of over two years he had not advanced far from grade 7, the lowest and entering grade, and few privileges had been his.

His mother had come to see him on the first opportunity available to her, the first Tuesday in July just over seven months after he had been sent from home. He never saw or heard from her again. He often wondered, especially in later life, what happened and why he never heard from his mother after that first visit. This loss that was never explained cast an added shadow over his life. He was now indeed a child of the state, and never found trace of a living relative.

4

Although he had only recently passed his fifteenth birthday, he was ready to be sent to an employer. It was now a matter of waiting until a man could be found in the country who was of sound character, who wanted a lad to work, who would give him lodging and food, and who would pay a little pocket money and a small amount into a trust account for his use when he came of age. At last such an employer was found.

The lad was called before the officer in charge and told that on the north coast of New South Wales there was a kind man who was prepared to give him a home on a farm, in return for the help he could render. He would also be given pocket money, and further wages would be banked for his future use. Would he like to go?

'Yes,' he replied, feeling it would be nice to have a home on a farm where he received payment.

He was told that the good name of the institution was now dependent upon him and that any failure of his part would reflect upon others and be regarded as a serious reflection upon his own character.

Such preliminaries being over, he was taken to Central Railway Station and put on a train going north. It was about a twelve-hour journey. With a sigh of relief, he found himself alone on the train, and not least of that relief was the freedom from what seemed to him a prison with frightening discipline.

Train travel was a new experience. Grit from the engine made his eyes smart and dirtied his face, but it was nice to be important enough to have a ticket for the journey and a seat all his own on the train. As he looked through the train window, the fields were large and green and just wonderful. The creeks and the rivers were so full of water that he would have liked to play by them all day. The bush was so thick and the trees so large that he imagined himself hiding from everyone among them. How beautiful the cattle looked as they fed or rested among the lush grass. This was different, he would never go near Sydney again. Then he went into a reverie. What sort of people would he meet…kind people, they said… perhaps someone who understood like his mother… The train rattled along as he dreamed his dreams. The towns seemed more friendly as he looked at them, and the people on the stations didn't really frighten him. He had a ticket and a seat on the train that was his very own, and he was going to kind people, and he was going to work and earn money for himself: he wouldn't waste it like his father did.

With thoughts like this, he went to sleep. The train was not crowded and he spent the night hours easily, for the most part sleeping, sometimes dreaming of the cattle, the rivers, the bush and the ship with its officers that he had left behind forever. Once they were mixed together and he was running past the cattle into the bush, with the officers in close pursuit. Soon he knew he would have to jump into the river and swim for it. He plunged in and woke up frightened, but greatly relieved to find himself dry, safe, and still on the train.

Then he was asleep again, and only awakened at sunrise – an hour before it was time for him to alight at Tenterfield. The coach that was to take him further would not be leaving for another two or three hours, and the stationmaster showed him the rest room where he could wait. He was grateful for this kindness and being only half awake he spent the time in fitful sleep.

Later in the morning, he purchased a meat pie and a cup of tea at the railway refreshments rooms, and then the coach arrived and he, following other passengers, clambered aboard for the trip across country.

The roads were rough, sometimes just dirt, sometimes rough stones badly water-washed, with dangerous gutters that compelled the driver to brake suddenly and very slowly travel over the dangerous parts. But the roughness of the ride did not worry him; he enjoyed it. He would soon be at his new home, and that mattered most of all. Not even the hope of a new home could absorb his thought all the time. The horses amazed and delighted him. They were not as heavy as his father's horses had been, and the driver didn't swear at them either. Indeed, there was no need to curse them for they were clean-stepping and quick and seemed to anticipate the driver's wishes. At a sparkling stream across the roadway they stopped and drank thirstily, then paused in their drinking and after that pause, drank a little more. The driver did not hurry them from the water, and let them travel steadily for a time after the watering. The boy's only regret was that he could not alight at the stream to paddle and drink too. There was a passing flash of thought that having driven his father's horses, he might someday even have a job as a coach driver.

5

It was a happy but weary and begrimed youth who arrived at the farm late in the afternoon. He was shown to his room, a little room, containing a single stretcher bed and a small table on which stood a mirror. A chest of drawers completed the furniture, except for an empty corn sack placed flat on the floor beside his bed to be used as a mat. He was then shown to the wash house and told to have a good wash before tea, which would be ready soon. The wash house was a room with a bare wooden floor, and a tap coming to the room from an outside tank. Its only furniture was an old-style wooden wash stand on which rested a tin dish for washing. Another corn sack was on the floor in front of the stand, and a few large nails were in the wooden uprights of the unlined room for holding a towel or clothing.

The door of the wash room opened onto a back veranda, which made it easy to throw out the dirty water on to the yard. He soon learned that water came from a galvanised tank holding 1,000 gallons, that this came off the roof when it rained, and that with such an uncertain supply, water must be used sparingly. In emergency, water could be brought by horse and cart in milk cans from creeks running through the farm. This of course meant extra work and time taken from regular tasks, which led to extra care with the tank supply. Creek water was mostly hard, and also to some extent contaminated, and therefore its use was avoided as much as possible. All this about the use of water was impressed upon him early and he became as water-conscious as other members of the family.

After the clean-up, he had tea with the family in the kitchen. He found in the course of the next few days that he was always to have meals in the kitchen and even when the family had a meal in the dining-sitting room, he was served in the kitchen. At teatime this first evening, he was asked many questions about his early life and about the trip, but he was reserved and very shy and answered with 'yes' and 'no', except once he almost enthused about the journey by train and by coach.

When tea was over, he was told to go to bed and have a good rest, because he would be called at 6 o'clock in the morning to assist with the milking of the cows.

Before it was quite daylight and at exactly 6 o'clock he was called from bed, and life on the farm began in earnest. First he shared with the others the early morning snack, which consisted of a cup of tea and a slice of toast while sitting or standing around the kitchen table. The tea was made from a large kettle hanging on a hook from a dangling chain over the open fire, and the toast was made at the fire by each person using in turn the long homemade wire toasting fork. No time was wasted over this early cup of tea.

Father, who had brought in the cows, now returned and said, 'The cows are in,' and everyone bundled out to the cow yard and bails for milking while he made his toast and had a cup of tea before joining them.

Everyone else knew just what to do, but the boy felt and looked stupid and seemed to be in everyone's way. He had never seen so many cows – there seemed to be hundreds of them, though indeed there were about eighty – but being in three adjoining yards they seemed endless in number. Those that were close to him did not appear friendly but rather to ignore him, and he had a sense of feeling inferior to the cows as well. He felt suddenly afraid and confused. He was afraid of cattle and awed by these men who attended and controlled the cattle so easily. He was told to bail up cows and have them ready to milk, but he just stood, quite unable to act. Before long, the exasperated farmer called him stupid and this made him more afraid and less able to understand. Slowly and with much fear, he learned to drive cows into the bail and fasten them for miking. The cows had to be fastened in a bail, a leg rope was then used to prevent them from kicking, and a three-legged stool was in position for the men to sit and do the milking by hand.

At the first afternoon milking, a cow kicked him on the leg as he went past. He thought his leg was broken. But the others only laughed loudly at the incident. They had suffered the same, and had learned to be careful without any outward sign of care. Besides, only a few cows kicked, and they knew when care was needed. They laughed at him when he tried to milk and couldn't get any milk. They laughed at him when he slipped over in the muddy yard. It was not unkindly laughter. They felt that every experience was necessary, and would help him to pick up the work quicker, but what they didn't understand was the lad's background, his fear and terrible sense of inferiority which were increased by everything that went wrong.

Often in those first weeks, the farmer harassed with much work and little income, grumbled and threatened to report him as incapable, and said that he couldn't keep him there for ornament and pay him unless he learned more quickly to do work and earn his keep.

The boy completely lost confidence and thought of running away. He lay awake at night planning how to get away, but he knew so little about the country that for a time his plans were only wild dreams. At last, his opportunity came, and he took it.

One Saturday, the farmer and his wife and a man working on the farm all went to town. He was instructed to get the cows in early and start the milking if they were not home. No sooner were they gone than he gathered his few belongings in a small bundle and, taking some food from the cupboards, he ran away. He decided to walk a few miles and then hide in the hills over the weekend and later make for a town about twenty miles away, where he would enquire for work.

On retuning in the afternoon, the farmer was annoyed to see the cows were not herded for milking. When the state-boy did not answer his angry calls, he became anxious, but on going to the boy's room he knew at a glance what had happened because the little bits of clothing had all gone. Later, he missed some food from the kitchen. There was nothing he could do about it just then. Telephones were unknown in the country and, besides, the milking must be attended to at once. It was already late.

By Sunday, the report was around that the lad had stolen many things from his employer and had run away. The whole neighbourhood was on the lookout for the no good state-boy who had turned out to be a thief. Unfortunately, this rumour of theft was readily accepted and enlarged upon, because occasionally a state-boy with a bad background did turn out to be unreliable and a thief.

Meanwhile, he had rested part of Saturday and Sunday, and on Sunday afternoon set off towards the town, although he really did not know the way. Sunday evening turned wet and cold and his food had given out.

On Monday, cold and damp, he pressed on until the afternoon, when he decided to call at a home for something to eat.

The lady of the house, feeling sorry for him said, 'Yes, come in and out of the wet, and I'll get your something. Sit down by the fire and get warm and your clothes will dry a bit too, they look quite wet.' She gave him a glass of milk and asked, 'Where are you going?'

Not having thought out an answer, he replied simply, 'Nowhere.'

'But you must be going somewhere and it's getting late, too.'

'Oh', he answered, 'nowhere in particular. I'm looking for a job.'

To which she replied, 'I'm sorry, we can't afford to give you work. Where are you from?'

This time he was alert, but avoided telling a lie by saying, 'I came from Sydney and I've been out here a while.'

She queried, 'Been with friends?'

To which he answered, 'No, I've been working here.'

The woman did not pursue the questioning further. She set the bread and meat before him and noticed that he began to eat almost ravenously. Looking at him, she wondered what it was that was different about this lad. He was small and didn't look more than fourteen years, and couldn't be more than sixteen at the most, although he said he came from Sydney and had been working in the country, and was now looking for another job. He looked honest, and he was hungry. He must be in trouble of some sort. He wore a heavy grey suit too, much too large for him, and of quite different material and cut from those worn by the local boys.

Then she remembered rumours of a boy who had stolen things and had run away from a farm further up the river. She had taken little notice of the rumours. She decided to ask no further questions. Her husband would be home soon and she would talk to him about the lad. In the meantime, she invited him to remain by the fire for a while, saying, 'My husband will be home soon, and he may know about something for you.'

She heard her husband come into the yard and went out to meet him.

After a hurried conversation which the boy could not follow, they came into the kitchen together and the husband said bluntly, 'So you're the boy who has run away.'

The lad at once broke down and with tears running down his cheeks he begged, 'Don't give me up, I can't go back, I'm afraid they'll belt me.'

The man said sternly, 'They tell me you stole things when you left.'

'I didn't steal things,' he said, 'true, I didn't, I wouldn't steal things. I only took some food. You won't send me back, will you?' He pleaded. 'I'm afraid.'

Somehow the boy had convinced the husband that he was speaking the truth, and tears were trickling down the cheeks of his wife, who tried to make the position easier by saying as she wiped her eyes, 'I'll get tea ready and we'll see what we can do.'

'But you *won't* send me back, will you?' he pleaded again.

'We're not against you, and we'll see what can be done to help you,' said the not-unkindly husband as the wife busied herself getting tea. 'You can stay with us tonight, and we'll see what tomorrow brings.'

The whole family was friendly and avoided further embarrassing questions as they chatted over tea. Having promised not to run away, he was given a comfortable bed for the night.

He never forgot the short stay at their home, with the two boys, one about his own age and one a few years younger, and a small girl of six or seven years. They treated him as one of themselves and he wanted in his heart to stay with them always. Indeed, that night, feeling sorry for the boy and liking his straightforwardness and apparent honesty, they discussed the possibility of giving him employment. But with a small property, a large debt and their own three children to provide for, they could not afford to employ anyone, however small the immediate wage.

Soon the police called on a round of enquiry. The report had come to them that a state-boy had absconded after taking from the home of his employer. It became the duty of the police to make a search and they were calling at all farmhouses to enquire if anyone had seen the truant thief, in the hope of gaining some information that would lead to his capture. Even his safety might be at stake, they said.

The sergeant was a kindly man, but he had a duty to perform. He knew that the lot of these lads was often not a happy one at the homes to which they were sent, and that faults could be on either side, and indeed were sometimes on both. With firmness and yet with considerable compassion, he escorted Alfred Sully to the police station, where he made arrangements for his return to the *Sabraon* in Darling Harbour.

During this time, the lad was in great fear for the future and watched for any opportunity to escape, but none was given him.

Once back at the *Sabraon*, he was severely reprimanded, placed in the lowest form 7, without any privileges, and kept under strict discipline.

6

After a further year aboard the *Sabraon*, during which discipline was maintained at a high level – a discipline that missed his need, and therefore did not help him at all – he was for the second time deemed ready to be sent to an employer.

Again he found himself journeying northward by train. Although he was more than a year older, he was filled with foreboding and fear. He still loved the country, and looked at its beauty with wide open eyes and with deep yearning, but he did not really enjoy the train journey because he was lonely, uncertain of himself and sure there would be trouble when they found he could not do the work. What sort of people would they be? His thoughts kept returning to his drunken father and the floggings he had received when his father was under the influence of drink. He remembered the *Sabraon* with its discipline, and he knew well this was his last chance, for that had been made very clear before he left the ship. He remembered the farmer and the cows, and how they had laughed at him because he could not manage them, and had become angry and called him stupid. He would be as honest and helpful as he could, but would they call him slow and stupid again? He became sure he would be a misfit. In this frame of mind, he decided that if necessary he would run away again, but this time if he did so, he would not be found.

At long last, the journey ended and his new employer, who had been to town with a load of pigs, took him home in the spring cart with its nauseating odour. It was late when they arrived at the farmhouse, and after some tea he was sent to bed in a little room built without lining but not without cracks on the end of the veranda. It was furnished like the earlier one, this being almost standard furnishing for the room of a farm employee. He slept soundly until breakfast time. After breakfast he was shown around and told about his duties, which included milking cows morning and evening.

Then turning to him the farmer said, 'I've heard reports of your being dull and slow and of your running away from your last home. I'm giving you another chance, but you'd better not run away because the dingoes eat lads who wander alone in the bush, and see this rope: if you don't work well, or if you attempt to run away, it'll be laid on your hide till you can't stand up and you'll wish you'd never been born.'

The lad looked at the rope and at the man. Fear came into his eyes and the resolution of work and obedience left him. Even the dingoes would not deter him. From that moment, he resolved to run away. He knew that he had to find out much about the country, and he must discover what the danger was from dingoes, and he must not be discovered, but as soon as he could he would run away. Besides, he was nearly two years older than when he tried to run away before and he knew more and he would travel much further before seeking work, and be ready with answers too. When the time came, he must not be caught.

During the months of preparation for flight, he yarded and milked cows, and under supervision split posts, mended fences, chopped wood, sharpened the axe, helped with the ploughing and occasionally drove a horse and cart. He was not efficient at any of these and the farmer grumbled continually, but he did learn something about cattle and general farm work, and he now knew that it lasted from daylight till dark, with sometimes an inside job at night such as husking corn.

There was no forty-eight-hour working week on the farm, and both farmer and state-boy worked anywhere between seventy-five and ninety-five hours a week. On Sunday it was generally only necessary work such as milking cows or feeding horses.

At long last, the opportunity came to escape from all this, and he did not hesitate to take it. He travelled far and quickly, fear keeping him away from homes. He had a little money and bought only cheap and necessary things. This way, his money lasted many days, and he travelled a long distance. Sometimes he was a little frightened at night when all was so quiet, or the quietness was suddenly broken by the creatures of the dark. His biggest fright came from what he learned later was a koala, which made a sound that was first like a groan from someone injured, and when joined by other koalas, the gully rang with deep guttural roars and echoes. Years later, he smiled over this when he thought of these gentle harmless creatures, but at the time it was frightening indeed and he kept still under his hessian covering. To make matters worse during these wanderings, he dreamt several times that he was being pursued and once that he had been caught.

Having travelled a great distance, he finally, with some trepidation, sought and received work on a farm. He was not discovered. What efforts were made to trace him he never knew. This time, both the farmer and his wife were patient and even occasionally gave words of praise when they saw that the lad was anxious to please them with his work. He accepted the routine of farm work with its early rising, miking of cows, feeding calves and pigs, catching, harnessing and driving horses. He learnt to plough, to use an axe well, to cut undergrowth with the brush-hook, to dig post holes and to strain wire, and he became an efficient workman at all of these tasks that had been so difficult at first. Ploughing he found hardest of all. Being small, it was difficult for him to hold the heavy single furrow plough in the ground, and several times when it struck a root he was thrown yards away and badly bruised by the solid iron handles. He was working hard; indeed, he had never worked so hard before. The wages were little more than his keep, because the farmer could not afford to pay a high wage. But never before had he been so contented, and he was determined to show his appreciation by doing every task that was required of him. Maybe some day he would even own a farm!

The farmer and his wife liked this straightforward honest lad around the place. He was very slow at every task but he was entirely trustworthy. He was always good-humoured and even laughed at his own misfortunes. They had assets in the farm, and with milk, eggs and meat, and their own vegetables, it cost them little to live. But they received precious little income in money, about £150 [$300] a year, and most of this went in paying interest to the bank on their £1,750 [$3,500] farm mortgage, advanced at 5% interest. They gave the lad his keep and a few shillings a week pocket money, but it was a strain to pay even that and more was out of the question. They were glad to have him, and he was happy to have a home with kindly people, and work that he could do. For the first time in his life, he was happy. Deep-seated fears and inhibitions were slowly giving way to a new-found confidence that after all he had a place in the community. He did not need much money because he seldom went out, and the farmer's wife mended and patched his few clothes and bought new ones with his money when the old were past mending, which was seldom. For years, he stayed with them.

The time came when their two boys grew to manhood and could manage the farm work. He rolled his few belongings in a bush blanket and, with mixed feelings of regret, adventure and pride, he started out on the track, not knowing where his next job would be, but with confidence that he could do many things. His needs were few, and he could do without much money. Because he was well over twenty-one years of age, he no longer had any fear of being hunted as the state-boy who had run away. He felt he had been forgotten long ago, and with his new freedom to travel and work, he could smile to himself on his escape, and feel a little proud of it. Such was the background of his life, and such was the amount of his training.

He was now a swagman or, if you prefer the term, a tramp. He had little past that counted, and the future was all unknown and troubled him not at all.

7

He travelled southward and kept inland. Sometimes he felt the desire for friendship of the home left far behind. Occasionally he even felt all alone. These desires were mostly satisfied by the friendly spirit shown by swagmen he met almost every day on the roads, and by talks around the campfire with fellow workmen at night. With surprising quickness, he became at home with nature and liked the never-ending crooked roads, with their long straight stretches, and the days with their surprises, and the nights with the campfire and the stars and the sleep that was always very close to a tired man of the roads. Each morning he awoke with freshness and strength for the travel of the next day.

At this time too, he had gained something that other people seldom associate with the tramp. He felt that on the long roads, the quiet starry nights, and even the days of toil, that he was not alone, that God was near. People like you and me would say that he had little to be thankful for and that his lot was a hard one. But he was a happy man, with a dearly won freedom and a strength to earn his living.

On the New England roads, he received both rebuffs and kindness. Calling at homesteads for work, he was given at least a cup of tea and some food. Mostly it was offered with a kindly word, and he often cut some wood while they were getting the cup of tea. Sometimes he was given a job for a day, a week, a month, or occasionally for a year. Sometimes he slept in a back room or a shed but more often in a bark hut or tent. He was often cold, but learned to keep a fire burning night and day in winter weather. Wood could be had for the cutting and cost nothing, and even the cutting of it kept him warm. Besides, he was an excellent axeman who could cut straight and clean with his axe that had a keen edge.

The work varied in kind and included felling trees, brushing undergrowth and suckering, clearing land of logs by burning off, or digging out roots to get land ready for ploughing. Sometimes it was work with cattle such as mustering, branding, and even milking. He did not like the milking, and he was never a good horseman, although he learned to muster cattle reasonably well. Another time, it was ploughing, or gardening and the thrill of achievement in growing vegetables. Sometimes the work was cutting thistles, and in later years digging out rabbits or in harvest time sewing the tops of wheat bags as they were filled with the newly harvested crop. He was frequently employed splitting posts and putting up wire fences, or replacing rotted posts and repairing broken fences.

It was during one of these repair jobs that an eye was slightly injured by the recoil of a broken strand of wire during straining. He was far from aid and it seemed a small thing, but it led to serious trouble and the loss of sight in the eye. He never had medical attention for it. He had no money to seek it and there was no one who understood or cared enough to see if the eye could be saved. From then on, the sightless eye had a white appearance.

For these many and varied jobs, he received little more than his keep, but that little was not wasted and it helped to buy more working clothes. Wages were low because some landowners were mean, also because some were struggling hard to make ends meet. Much work was done by contract, and contract work was low-paid work, and besides he was a steady, reliable but slow worker.

Patching and mending of clothes, if done at all, was done by himself. Now and then, he would be given a pair of working trousers or a coat, but they never fitted and were always much too big, giving him the appearance of being even smaller and untidy as well.

During these years, he had been working south towards Armidale. It was then that he decided to carry his swag to Kempsey and the coast. The road was mountainous, very narrow, winding and dangerous. This did not give him much trouble, because motor cars were at the time almost unknown and were unlikely to attempt such a road. But it was an experience that he never forgot, because at one stage he was suddenly frightened and felt that he would never find the next water or a home where he could get a drink. On that trip he received no work and was often hungry. He was used to that, but this first experience of thirst was a frightening thing that he remembered to his dying day. Unexpectedly, he had travelled all through the hot day in mountainous country without finding water or sighting a home. He became tired and weak, and plodded along with a sense of fear and despair growing. No one was travelling on that road. He would be too weak to continue walking next day if he had to spend the night without water.

Seeing a gully that looked a likely place, he decided in desperation to seek water there. Leaving the road, he took off his coat, placed it on his swag and hid them behind a rock. He then went down over sharp broken stones, but found no water. The gully looked like producing water further on, so he went further. For the best part of an hour, he continued on and on until the gully flattened out and water seemed further off than ever. He knew that his judgement had been wrong and he had come down a dry gully. Why had he been so foolish? Precious time had been wasted and strength expended. Perhaps a traveller who would have helped him had passed by along the road. He sat down bewildered by his position. In the heat of the afternoon, he now felt weak and, looking back towards the road, it could not be seen. Fear gripped. Was he lost, and had he lost his swag too? It would turn cold here at night, and he had no matches, and there was no water.

The fear was momentary. Then, trying to be calm, he stood up and looking around endeavoured to get his bearings. With the passing of sudden panic, he thought that he recognised the gully through which he had travelled and knew that by following it back he must, if strength lasted, come at last to his swag and the road. Stumbling sometimes over stones and slipping on steep places, he at last knew it was the right gully and he reached the swag by the roadside. Exhausted, he sat on the swag, took matches and tobacco from his coat which had been left under the swag and made himself a cigarette. For fifteen minutes he relaxed there, and then felt the urge to push on further before sunset in the hope of finding water by the roadside or perhaps even yet meeting a traveller or sighting a home. Scrambling back to the road, he adjusted the swag to his back and continued his way.

Towards sunset, he could have shouted for joy when he saw another tramp coming towards him. This man was older and more experienced in bushcraft, and knew this part of the country. He told him about a spring in the bush about two miles further on and one hundred yards from the road. After listening very carefully to directions, Sully pressed on and found water just as darkness came. Though still hungry after the last crust of bread was eaten, he was contented and, lighting a fire, camped for the night.

A few days later, he was fortunate enough to receive work. Later he walked to the coast, a further twelve to fourteen miles, and looked on the sea for the first time in many years. He did not wish to stay there. It somehow reminded him of the years on the *Sabraon* and he was depressed. Never again did he seek employment on the coast. The appeal of the inland with its quietness, solitariness and kindness was so strong that he remained there all the days of his working life.

After a few months on the coast, he returned to Armidale by this same road, happy in the knowledge of the hidden bush spring on the long dry mountain stretch. This experience he regarded as one of his worst on the roads, and it was to him a warning to be careful about travelling unknown tracks without making enquiry about the presence of water. Indeed, he received a lesson through fear on this trip that prevented him from ever going into a waterless region unprepared.

He once said to me, 'I've been in many dry places, and travelled down many dry gullies, but that stretch on the Armidale–Kempsey Road caused my greatest panic, and that dry gully I followed was the one that frightened me most.'

Leaving Armidale, he passed Thunderbolt's Rock and camped at the first water beyond it. He always admired the courage of this bushranger, especially the holding of a coach load of people at the point of a revolver –

when the revolver was only a wooden dummy! Once he remarked to me, 'My word, he was game. Only had a dummy revolver, and they all stood there. They'd have torn him to pieces had they known.'

Sully had a quaint laugh that was always accompanied by a few unchecked tears as he really entered again into the experiences that he related. Like many Australians, he admired the sense of justice and gallantry of the bushranger, even though he recognised they were outside the pale of law and could not be allowed to continue. His vocabulary was simple and limited. He never made a habit of swearing or of using violent slang to emphasise a point, as so many Australian bushmen do, and it would have been impossible for him to blaspheme although he was in the thick of it most of his life.

Continuing southward, he worked on properties around Tamworth, Gunnedah, Coonabarrabran, Dubbo, Parkes, Forbes, Cowra, Galong. Binalong and Wagga, and went as far south as Albury by the river Murray and the Victorian border, but he seldom stayed long in one place. The call of the open spaces was now in his veins and he loved the open road. The road gave him a sense of elation and freedom. Here he owed no one anything, he was responsible to no one, and he was free to walk or rest or camp. He liked seeing the towns and the country. There was always a bridge or culvert near each town that provided shelter for camping, and in the country he looked for a creek or waterhole. He was never lonely and usually had a dog that was a mate in travel and company at night. The dog shared his food and spoken confidences.

Employers soon learned that the word of this man of the road could be relied upon, and that any job he undertook would be completed slowly but conscientiously. If ever an employer became exasperated, it was always for the same reason – he was a slow worker. He was never lazy, but he was slow and could not compete with the quickness of the general Australian worker on the land. He always rose before sunrise and generally at the break of day with the first laugh of the kookaburra.

Working by the sun in summer and winter, he knew when to cease work to allow just enough time for getting tea, and any other odd job such as cutting wood before dark. Generally he watched the darkness fall while enjoying an after-tea smoke. He rolled his own cigarettes, and rolled them well with intense deliberation. After the smoke, he went to bed. This habit continued even when he ceased from regular work, and without fail he was always about at daybreak and long before sunrise. He never spoke of the sunrise or the sunset, but accepted them as his clock, and enjoyed the sunrise for early rising and the sunset for late meditation. He never possessed a watch or a clock. The sun and the kookaburras were complimentary and sufficient.

8

Early in his experience as a tramp he erected a tent for a few nights near a waterhole on flat ground outside the town where he had been given some odd jobs of cutting wood and gardening. It was a dry season, but the grass was green at this spot, making it a handy and pleasing place to camp. One afternoon as he returned to the tent, he noticed heavy clouds that threatened an evening storm. He had tea and made sure the tent ropes were secure to pegs and trees, although in such a sheltered place there would not be much damage from wind. He crept into his bunk before the storm broke and was soon fast asleep.

Later in the night there was thunder and lightning and a deluge of rain that continued for hours. He half-woke to hear and see these, but they did not really disturb him.

In the early morning before daylight, he was awakened by a peculiar swishing sound. He listened, but it was not the wind. Wondering, he stepped out of bed, and his foot went into about six inches of water which was flowing strongly through the tent. It was a great shock, but it was too dark to see just what damage was done. The rain had stopped and with his blankets and few clothes he hastened from the water to higher ground, and finding an open shed that was reasonably dry he slept there until the first break of day. Returning at once to the tent, he found it still standing, and the bed erected with saplings fifteen inches above the ground was there but his billies and bits of food could not be found. The water was no longer flowing through the tent. The flood had come and gone with the darkness.

He just stood and looked wryly at the ruin, and at last a smile flitted across his face. He was working, and with the little bit of money due to him, the things lost could be replaced. He had become conscious of his own thoughtlessness and was contented to have escaped so lightly from this camp on green grass near the waterhole. He was a little bit ashamed of not knowing better than to pitch his tent on such low ground and in a dry waterway, and he did not tell the townspeople or seek their help. Seldom did he speak of this experience but he never again pitched his tent in a place that could be easily flooded in times of storm.

Indeed, after this experience he was not again caught in a flood large or small, although on one occasion while carrying his swag he came to Gundagai and found the Murrumbidgee so high that he could not cross the bridge, and had to camp for several days. On this occasion he saw the tremendous force of turbulent waters as, hemmed in by hills, they flowed through the town. Once through the town, the waters spread over miles of agricultural land, completely destroying crops and spreading debris a mile in width. At that time he stored away a thought in his mind: 'I must never be caught in a terrible flood like this.' And he never was.

Baker's bread was not always procurable. When it was, he did not mind whether it was fresh or stale, one day or a week old. But often there was no baker, and on these occasions he made 'puftalooners' and enjoyed them. The puftalooner was made with flour and water and a pinch of salt. Baking soda was used if available, but it was not regarded as essential. It was an extremely simple recipe which he did not write down, but remembered as follows: mix flour and water until thick and firm so as not to be sticky. Sprinkle a little flour over the dough and press or roll it flat. Cut into suitable sizes and drop into boiling fat in a frying pan. Take out when nicely browned. Eat when cool enough. In times of plenty, they were specially nice with golden syrup, honey or jam, or with meat. Nothing went so wrong with the cooking that it had to be thrown away. He liked them hot best of all, but he liked them cold the next day, or the day after if they were left, but that seldom happened.

For a change in camp cooking, he occasionally made a damper instead of puftalooners. The making of a damper had its own technique. Returning from work, he regularly stripped to the waist and with water in the all-purpose tin dish, he would have a quick splash wash. Then, throwing out the soapy water, he would rinse the dish with some clean water and proceed with making the damper. Firstly, flour would be placed in this same dish, and water with a little salt and baking soda added. With his hands, this was mixed into a stiff dough. The fire, burning all the day, would have some ash and red hot coals. Scraping them level, the firm dough well was sprinkled with flour, placed on them, and with a spade or piece of tin or bark, further coals and ashes were heaped upon it. In due time, these were removed and a brown appetising damper was taken up. Watching the whole procedure you might not have felt like eating it, but the tramp would eat it with relish and not a slice was wasted. Ashes and coals did not adhere to the damper, which came out surprisingly clean. I have tasted them, and apart from some prejudice as to the perfect cleanliness of the dish, they were really nice.

In times of drought, the rabbits became very destructive of the little grass left for the sheep, and often at such times his work was digging out rabbits from their burrows. Sometimes when they were really plentiful, he received no wages but was able to support himself from the sale of skins, using a few traps to increase his catch. When he first took on rabbiting, one farmer offered him ten pounds for the last rabbit on his property, but Sully soon dropped to this leg pull and told the farmer it was no use pulling his leg that way. The reply was, 'It's no leg pull, and it would be worth a lot more than ten pounds to me if you could exterminate the rabbits on my property.' The last one was never caught, and the ten pounds was never paid, but at least it was a standing goodwill joke between them.

Drought time was also fire time, and he would proudly say, 'Never once did a fire get away from me and cause any damage.' In camping during summer time, it was essential to be near permanent water and away from a dangerous fire hazard or fire trap. The tramp had only his own fire sense between him and death during extensive bushfires. In summer, the ground around his tent and fireplace was kept clear of grass or other burning material.

He was first made fire-conscious by seeing the ploughed firebreaks around inland homesteads and crop paddocks and even properties.

These were usually ploughed six or more feet wide, and sometimes he was employed ploughing these breaks or checking them. Bushfires that neither firebreaks nor local fire fighting brigades could control had caused him to fear and respect this kind friend and cruel enemy of men. He would say, 'Some men are never safe with matches. Can't resist lighting little fires. They just don't know how it can spread like a flash all around them in really dry conditions. A puff of wind comes and it's out of their control, and all they can do is to get out of its way. Or they may light a cigarette and throw the match down and it does not go out as expected, or they throw away a cigarette butt that's still alight and somehow it comes to rest on dead bark or twigs or dead grass, and a fire starts minutes later, perhaps unknown to them.'

That fire once started cannot be stopped by one man on a windy day in the dry tinder of drought time, even if he sees it at the beginning. It may cause thousands of pounds of damage, the loss of hundreds of stock, and often the loss of many lives by exhaustion in firefighting or by being trapped and burned. He remembered one man who had lost control of his own fire and who, because of a sudden change in the direction of wind, was half-blinded by smoke and died in the flames. He had seen fires caused by railway engines, and claimed that others were started by bottles and storms in hot weather, but mostly fires came from the carelessness of some person.

9

He never suffered loneliness in the bush or countryside and found its natural inhabitants very interesting. Often, birds used to frequent his tent. They were never molested and were encouraged with crusts of bread. When he had a dog, it was inclined to be jealous and would not allow the birds to settle on the ground. At such times, they perched in the trees around the tent until Sully went to work followed by the dog. They then came for the crusts and showed no fear as they hopped around the tent, mostly in silence, but sometimes chattering and occasionally fighting over a special titbit.

He liked the kookaburra best of all. It was his clock, laughing as the darkness fell and laughing again when the break of day was scarcely discernible to human eyes. Sometimes a number of them would roost in an old tree near his tent, and in the nesting season a pair would enter the hole of a broken branch and lay their white eggs. Occasionally a pair would peck their way into a white ants nest high in the tree and there lay their eggs and rear their young. He had even seen them nesting in a high perpendicular mud bank of the Murrumbidgee, where they had pecked a neat suitable hole.

He occasionally noticed a kookaburra sitting on a branch concentrating its gaze on the ground without the slightest movement. Then suddenly it would fly straight down thirty or even sixty feet and return with a mouse in its beak. After sitting contentedly in the branch for a few seconds, it would bash the mouse a couple of times on the branch and swallow it. Two or three times only did he notice kookaburras do this with small snakes, mostly about twelve to eighteen inches long. On such occasions, there was more care taken with the killing, and the snake would be bashed on a solid branch for up to ten minutes. These snakes were mostly venomous varieties, black or brown.

One morning he saw a kookaburra sitting on a rail of a fence fully concentrating on something in the grass. It was close by his tent. Walking quietly up to the bird from behind and placing his hand on its back and wings, he quietly lifted it off the fence. It was clearly surprised, as he held it firmly, but it made little protest. In a soft voice which it seemed to understand, he called it 'My pretty little bird' and thanked it for killing mice and snakes. Placed on the fence again, it immediately flew away.

He always had a kind thought for the blue wren and its little brown mate, and did not fail to notice the occasional red one, admiring their restlessness in search of food, and their airy lightness of movement. The peewit too was a favourite with its black and white beauty and its queenly step. The currawong thrilled him with its call and its activity and swooping flight as it sought berry food, especially on showery days. They ate the bread crusts he occasionally threw to them, and their presence in large numbers was to him a sign of clearing after rain.

The crow he did not like because of its cruelty in attacking lambs and dying sheep, but with bush philosophy he would say, 'I s'pose they have their uses.'

He had seen brolgas dancing towards sunset, and in describing their lightness and beauty he tried to imitate them. I shall never forget the little old short-sighted man and his grotesque attempt to dance and bow like the native companion, but I had seen them too and his attempt was well made.

Another bird he mentioned to me was the curlew, with its eerie night call. It was regarded as a companion of the night. Several times while clearing paddocks of suckers and undergrowth, he came upon them in pairs and, being night birds, they were slow to move in the day. But even in the day standing with their long legs and long necks with the colouring of the brown surroundings, he found them difficult to discern until they moved.

Once in heavier brush he came across a dingo with two pups. The pups were active, but the dingo did not seek to escape until the pups were collected, and then she quietly and quickly disappeared with them in the timber.

The wallaby and the kangaroo were distant friends, and often he greeted them as they hopped quietly by, or as they stopped to gaze at the bushman, or went bounding past with the tremendous hops of flight.

The opossum was a friendly marsupial too, and its eyes shone like balls of light when caught in the reflection of the campfire at night. It always came at night and had a liking for cold tea and scraps of bread and cheese. He learned to keep food out of its way, and he did not mind it looking around for scraps and occasionally disturbing his sleep by overturning a billy or some such mishap. At daybreak it was never seen, having returned to sleep in the hollow branch of a nearby tree.

He never used a gun, and apart from rabbits never injured these bush friends.

Later, while he was living at Mudgee with me, we had a strange bird experience. One morning, we had thrown out a slice of bread for birds, and were sitting talking. At this time of day, a pair of magpies often came for bread. One of them was large, a glossy black and white, while the other was smaller and dingy black and white. The larger one had always arrived first.

On this day, the smaller bird came first and was quietly eating the slice of bread. Then the larger one arrived. He surveyed the scene for five or ten seconds, then edged up and pulled the other's tail. She kept eating and ignored the tail-pull. Next, he came closer and took her leg in his beak, but again he was ignored while the smaller bird kept eating. Then coming closer still he bumped her and she, losing balance, fell over. Thereupon he stepped on her outstretched wing and himself started eating the bread. After a mouthful or two, he released her wing, and she quietly arose and walked about two feet away. He continued his meal, and when finished walked away. Then the smaller bird returned and finished her meal, after which they both flew away one behind the other. This was all done quietly, and with no sign of agitation. It was something I would not have believed had it not happened in my presence, and apparently we saw a law of bird land being applied at its best.

Sometimes snakes gave him a fright. They were around in spring, summer and autumn, although as a general rule not very numerous. The black and brown were the most plentiful inland, but in the earlier years on the coast he had seen the diamond, the carpet, the whip, the green, the banded snake and the deaf adder.

One evening, he received a hair-raising fright by stepping on a carpet snake which he mistook for another dead sapling lying on the ground in timbered country. He later remarked, 'I'm glad it wasn't a black one. He'd have been too quick for me although I made a record jump.' The largest carpet snake he had seen was ten feet long.

Many farmers kept a carpet snake in the barns to destroy rats that ate the corn, and before camping in a barn he always asked if there was a rat-catcher there. On one such occasion, the farmer lost a pup. The carpet snake was found coiled up soundly asleep with an ominously large swelling in its abdomen. The snake was killed on suspicion, and when it was opened, there was the dead pup intact. Somehow it had been closed in the corn shed, and had become a victim of the rat-catcher.

He occasionally disturbed snakes in logs and under rubbish or stooks of hay. Once while digging thistles beside a decaying log, he dug out a snake with a couple of young six- or nine-inch snakes, and also several eggs. The snake was not very active but the mother snake at once swallowed a young one near her. He killed them, and broke the two soft-shelled eggs to discover young snakes in different stages of fertilisation. This was a whip snake.

One other incident with the whip snake is worth recording. Hearing a frog croaking in what was plainly a fear or distress call just off the bush track, he went to investigate. There he saw the snake with the frog swallowed to the middle of its body. The frog was thicker by far than the body of the snake and it was calling in terror as it was being slowly swallowed from behind.

There was one snake incident in the early years which he never forgot. Coming back from dinner, he saw a five-foot brown snake sunning itself in front of the tent. He hurried to the wood heap for a long stick, and lost sight of the snake for a few seconds. Finding a suitable stick, he hurried softly back, only to find the snake had disappeared. Had it gone into the bush or into the tent? If it had gone into the bush, he might never see it again, but if it had gone into the tent, it could be very dangerous. Looking carefully, he suddenly saw it coiled around one of the pieces of sapling driven into the ground to support his bunk. Looking closely, he could see beady treacherous brown eyes intently watching him from a covered place beneath the middle of the coil. The bunk was partly in the way, and so was the tent itself, which was scarcely six feet high in the centre and only four feet where the snake coiled.

He raised the stick as high as possible and edged into the best position for striking. He dared not hesitate for long, and with only a four-foot drop, he struck a blow with as much force as he could muster. As he jumped back, the snake uncoiled in a flash. As it moved and lashed about viciously, he noticed with relief that in one place about three feet from the head there was no movement. This lack of movement came from a broken back. Because of the bed, he could not at once hit it again. In its frenzy, the snake twice bit itself, but soon it became quieter and he tried to manoeuvre it into a better position for killing. He went too close, and suddenly three feet of snake shot out at him so quickly that he could not move away in time. That vicious strike was only inches short of his leg and after he had finally killed it, he was trembling and almost exhausted. Had it bitten him, he was far from assistance and his life would have depended upon the success of his own immediate treatment.

Such were the hazards of the bush. He accepted them and learned to use every possible care.

In the Riverina one summer afternoon, a perfect mirage greeted him, and there a mile away was a lovely expanse of water out of which were growing quite large she-oak and Murray pine trees. It was so realistic that he just couldn't believe that the water and trees were not there until on coming closer the vision receded and then disappeared.

Twice he took the job of a rouseabout at a shearing shed. This involved yarding sheep, having a few in the pen ready for the shearers, carrying fleeces away, making cups of tea, indeed being everywhere and being quick about it. Occasionally he was called on to kill and dress a sheep for the shed, and this he could do well, although it was a task he did not like. When anything went wrong, the rouseabout was to blame, and he was called slow, stupid, an idiot, and many profane names which were spoken sometimes in good will and sometimes with venom.

Wages were better than he was used to, although some of the shearers earned four times as much, but he did not like the rush of the sheds and he left at the end of a fortnight. The first time he undertook this work, it was in a hand-shearing shed. He tried it once more a few years later and this time the shearing was done by machine clippers. The pace was even quicker and the noise greater. Not liking this hectic life, he again left after a couple of weeks and never returned to a job as rouseabout at a shearing shed.

He was very interested in the way that a ewe sheep could call her lamb. In a yard of a thousand sheep, a ewe would be completely separated from her lamb, yet when the ewe bleated, the lamb would answer, and although there might be hundreds of ewes bleating and hundreds of other lambs answering, in the course of ten or fifteen minutes the ewe and her lamb would be together. He would say, 'Those sheep must know more than I do, because they all sound much alike to me and hundreds seem to be bleating at once.'

There was other work to do on sheep and cattle stations such as clearing land of noxious weeds, and suckers, or burning off logs and other rubbish. Sometimes he undertook to clear land by the acre, but seldom made more than food from these contracts.

A milestone was the day a mailman fell ill, and the call came to him to drive the two horses tandem and deliver mail and parcels on the forty-mile run. I can still see the pride on his open face in the telling as he thrilled to the drive, and tears trickled down his cheeks as again he held the reins and had a foot on the brakes, and again delivered the mail safely for the sick man. Such responsibility was seldom his and it was an achievement never to be erased from his memory. Tears came easily to him as his eyes sparkled with pride and merriment over an achievement such as this.

Being easy to get along with, there were yet standards to which he strictly adhered. Honesty was one of these. Others were freedom of thought, freedom to come and go, freedom to go about a job in his own way, and an intense dislike of bossing. He would not argue, but if one was alert, a hurt look could be seen in his brown eye and flashing across his face. When this happened, unless there was something very important to hold him, he would quietly pack his swag that night and be on the road long before sunrise the next day with the grey blanket neatly and securely wrapped around his long swag which hung easily and lightly on his back supported by a padded shoulder strap. If reasonably possible, the money owing was collected before he left, but if not he went without it. A word of appreciation spoken when a job was finished never failed to bring a sparkle of pleasure to his eye. He knew that the task had been conscientiously done, but maybe not that he was a slow worker.

10

In the summertime, the flies are hard to live with in the sheep and cattle country. They breed by the thousand in the manure near the sheds, and in the heat of the day they are lazy and sticky and are intolerable to the man at work with his hands. To the man travelling by road and carrying things in both hands, they become unbearable. Sully had been told often of wearing a hat with corks hanging from the brim by strings. He had seen other tramps wearing them. Having some money, he purchased a cheap sombrero hat and tried hanging corks on it which came down from the brim about four inches and hung about level with the nose, six corks in all. This was surprisingly successful. Unless the wind was blowing strongly from behind, scores of flies would settle on the back and remain there. The corks on the hat provided a resting place for the odd fly that was disturbed and otherwise would have settled on his nose or about his eyes in a sticky and determined way.

This hat served him well for several years until one day, as he was walking close to the Murrumbidgee River near Harden, a sudden gust of wind lifted the hat from his head and carried it swiftly along the road. Hurrying after the hat, he had almost retrieved it when another gust sent it swirling away. It was then he noticed the wind had formed a willy-willy which, with the hat, was going directly to the bank of the river. Seeing the danger, he moved as fast as the swag would let him, but the willy-willy had taken control of the hat and whirled it over the river bank and out of sight.

When he came to the river, the hat had disappeared, and the willy-willy too had gone as suddenly as it had come. Standing still and gazing up and down stream, he suddenly saw the sombrero in the water a few feet from the edge and against a dead branch that had broken from a tree.

A log enabled him to almost reach it and then, putting one foot carefully on a smaller log, it was within his grasp. Just as his fingers touched it, the smaller log moved, and he slipped off it feet first into the deep water. Rising through the water, his head hit the underside of the log, and for the moment he had the feeling of being trapped beneath it. A second later, he came gasping to the surface and, grabbing the firm log, he clambered hastily out of the water and back to dry land. Looking for the hat, he saw it being carried slowly downstream by the current. Would it come to the bank again?

As he watched, it was carried further and faster by the current, and then nearing a bend in the river it moved towards the opposite bank, where finally it was caught in the fine branches of a partly submerged tree. It being a lonely part of the river, he took off the wet boots and socks. Placing the boots upside down to drain, he wrung the water from the socks. Then removing his grey flannel shirt, he wrung the water out of that and put it on again. Finally removing the trousers, he wrung them and completed dressing. Somewhat exhausted, he sat down, partly to rest and partly to watch for any movement of the hat. It soon became clear that the sombrero with its corks was securely caught in the branches and so, gathering up the swag, he returned to the road and continued on his way.

When asked why he did not swim the river and rescue the hat, the reply came at once. 'I'm not much of a swimmer and the river was wide and deep, and besides there were many snags, and it seemed better to lose the old hat than get drowned.' He solaced himself by soliloquising, 'I had it a long time and it was almost worn out.'

From his description, it really was 'holey' worn. From this time, he decided to travel with at least one hand free. By tying billies and other extras to his swag, he managed to do so. In his free hand he carried some leafy twigs, about eighteen inches long, and bashed the flies that were in front and sometimes those that were behind – but generally speaking those that were behind were unmolested because, disturbed, they became a greater nuisance. This method demanded energy, but early in the day it was exhilarating, though later it was only the determined fly on the face that was listlessly brushed aside.

Because of a love for the road, it was not unusual to travel for a couple of weeks before really seeking a new job. Needs were few and a little flour and some tea in the billy were sufficient to complete the contentment that came with freedom. If tea was short, and shops were many miles away or money was scarce, he would call at a roadside homestead, and the humble little shy man with the frank open face and quiet smile was seldom denied. Until ready, he would not ask for work, but if it was offered and the person was friendly, and he felt that he could do the work, and there was a shed or a bark hut available, he would accept it. Being satisfied with the job offered, the price for the job and the accommodation, he would place the swag in the hut, and look around for a fireplace either inside or outside.

If the accommodation was a hut and the fireplace was inside and it smoked, he did not really care. The smoke would drive away mosquitoes and other insects which could be much worse than smoke. If there was no hut, and the job was to last for months, he would erect a tent. In it, a bed was quickly made without cost by placing two crossed sticks in the ground, one pair for each end of the bed. Then two long and sturdy poles were put through the corners of two corn sacks and placed longways from end to end in such a way that the weight of the body tautened the sacks for comfortable sleeping. Such a bed took but little space, only about two feet six inches by six feet, and was wonderfully restful for a tired man. In tents, they were the accepted thing, and in the cottage tent and fly which was in general use, the bed fitted along one of the low sides which could not otherwise be used much.

Sometimes, as an alternative, two forked sticks were driven into ground at each end of the bed and nearly three feet apart. With two at each end, and the six-foot poles on the forks, the chaff sack again would make a comfortable bed. But the forks must be prevented from coming together and so collapsing the bed or making it uncomfortable. This meant securing cross sticks to the forks at each end.

The camp being prepared by about midday, he would proceed to cook a frugal meal. The rest of the day was used making a rough table out of the common kerosene case and setting out his plate, knife and fork, billycan and any other camping accoutrement on it, ready for constant use. The top boards from the case were taken off and nailed to the four corners to keep the case about eighteen inches off the ground and on its side so as to form a more or less firm and comfortable table. The case in this position also served as cupboard to hold a tin of jam, some salt, sugar, tea, dripping and perhaps bread or other food. Meat had to be kept on a tin plate in a flour bag or sugar bag to keep it away from the blowflies. In the summertime, the meat would keep only little more than a day. Ants were kept away by placing the jam or other tin in a plate of water, or even by standing the four legs of the kerosene box table in tins of water. The camp supply of water was generally kept in a four-gallon kerosene tin which was refilled when empty. The tin was prepared by having the top cut out and a wire-loop handle inserted.

The home being ready, he would cut a little wood, and sharpen his tools with the whetstone with which he was adept. The whetstone was slow work, but time did not matter and he always persisted until the edge was such that it would shave the hair from his arms. An axe entrusted to him was always in good hands and finally returned in good order and sharp condition. Sometimes when he was near the homestead, a grindstone was available, and as it was nearly always fitted with a foot pedal for the convenience of turning and sharpening by one man, he would use it.

What was left of the day he would use for meditation on his handiwork and the enjoyment of an undisturbed smoke. This preparation might even take two days but, having all the time there was, he was not perturbed.

Soon after sunset, he would go to bed, and sleep the sleep of the contented. Never did I hear him complain of not being able to sleep, and such a thought probably never entered his mind.

In such a manner he spent the first day, and when necessary the second day, and developed a sense of belonging which made him ready and anxious for work the following morning.

Having almost completed a job at one homestead, he was offered a Border collie sheepdog. By simple kindness to the mother dog, he had gained her friendship, and out of goodwill the people offered him what was really a valuable pedigreed pup. At first he refused, not because he didn't want it, but because he had become so attached to previous dogs that when they died through accident or poisoning he became so distressed that he was reluctant to possess another. This pup was only a few weeks old and its coat was a shining black and it had a natural broad white ring around its neck. It would be difficult to look after on the track and he was putting himself in the way of being hurt again if anything should happen to it. The glossy coat and the pedigree finally won him. He accepted it, and he smiled and cuddled it with real affection as he took possession.

A month later, on leaving the homestead, he spoke a few words of sympathy to the mother dog ('the old lady' he called her), and turned towards the road. The pup was not easy to carry together with his swag, and a short way along the road he tipped out the cold tea that was in the billycan, dried it out with some dead grass and, placing more dead grass in the bottom, he then put the pup in the billy. This became its home in travel until they settled again for the next job. When the pup whined, he looked for shade or at least a comfortable place to sit at the roadside, tipped it out of the billy to crawl round for a while and then gave it a drink and some small scrap of food he had saved. He had all the time there was, and there was no occasion to hurry because the evening camp could be just here or four miles further on without either gain or loss. Time and distance were seldom of any consequence.

For weeks he carried the Border collie pup in that billycan and after the billy was washed at a creek or water hole or excavated tank or at a homestead, the tea brewed in it was still excellent – even better than before, because that billy had made it possible for him to carry his little friend, who now brought him constant joy as she tumbled round the camp.

Fortunately, in a month or two, he received a job of suckering and clearing a hundred-acre paddock and this work lasted for over a year and the pup grew big and strong and would never again fit into a billycan or need to be carried. This job was a hard and long one, lasting longer than expected. He did not make much money from it, but it provided a home, work, food and clothing, and he was satisfied.

The pup of the billycan had now become a grown dog. It had also become his companion of the campfire, the tent, the hut and the road; even more than that, it had grown to be his closest friend. The Border collie is not always a friendly dog, except to its master, and to him it is faithful until death. These two became inseparable. Every meal was shared faithfully, even when that meal was a crust. She would walk silently beside him or behind him on the long trek of the road, and at night she would listen with attention while he recited events of the day or the plans for tomorrow. Often he chuckled at her rapt attention, and the dog's countenance brightened in response. She seldom barked at night, but kept guard carefully. If a disturbance continued, she barked quicker and retreated towards the master to awaken him and receive support.

11

It was late in the Depression that our paths crossed for the second time. He called on me at Mudgee, New South Wales. He was in distress, but even I could sense an independence in his quiet approach. At first I did not recognise him – nor he me, but slowly it dawned on me that years before we had met on the Coolamon–Ganmain Road where I had given him and the dog and the pup a lift in the car. Here was the little man of about five feet one inch, neither fat nor thin but of about medium build. The pup of years before was now a well matured dog, black with a natural collar of white hair which was sleek and shortish. The mother-dog had died, but how I was never told.

The tramp had not shaved for months, and a shaggy beard covered his face and came down to his chest. His greying hair hung down over the collar of an old serge coat. The coat had no elbows and had a large rent at the front and another larger one at the back. A grey flannel shirt was terribly thin, but no tears were visible. Even more noticeable were the trousers that were as much too big for him as the coat and seemed as though they might have belonged to it. The knees had been roughly patched but without avail. They were rent in other places, both in front and behind, and there was little that could be done about these worn parts – though the wear and tear could have been in even worse places.

His boots were of the light blucher type, turned up at the toes through being wet many times and dried out in front of the campfire. Later he lifted his foot, and without surprise I saw that some two inches square of the sole and inner sole were missing, and signs of paper and cardboard told their own tale of how he managed to walk in them at all. He did not have any socks. The crowning piece of all was an old felt hat with a mighty hole in the crown through which straggled unkempt greying hair.

He carried a long neatly rolled swag, the outward cover of which was a grey blanket and I noticed again that it was kept on his shoulders by a tidily padded strap.

At first he made no attempt to place the swag on the ground, but he did so later when I showed an interest and engaged with him in conversation. The dog was walking quietly behind him, and at first stood silently to attention. Later, it sat waiting and without movement beside the swag. In the face of all this disadvantage, he approached me with a humility supported by a natural dignity that he never lost even on difficult occasions.

The Depression which hit Australia in the late 1920s and continued throughout the 1930s was at its worst. He was not asking for food. He had just received his fortnightly ration at the Mudgee police station. He was not asking for clothes. He needed them, especially boots, and would have received them gratefully. What he did need badly was friendship, for the time had come when he sorely needed advice and help.

The years of travelling had not been conducive to either making or keeping friends. Now in time of dire need he was alone. He did remember a district where for five years he had worked. A squatter there had been helpful and could testify to his honesty. But years had passed and he was not sure of the name or of the address or even whether the squatter was still alive. He could have walked two hundred miles or more to the home, but names and addresses had never been of any consequence and therefore they were not remembered. This was a serious stumbling block in seeking a pension, for although he was confident of having reached the age of sixty-five years, which made him eligible for the age pension, he had no proof of age either from a birth certificate or by way of reference from old friends who had known him in youth. Never before had he felt so alone and so inadequate. He was up against a set of circumstances with which he could not cope. Because of the Depression throughout the country, there was no work, even for an experienced tramp who was prepared to work for little more than his keep.

Travelling between jobs, and especially during the years of depression, it was the custom of tramps and hundreds of others who were on the track to call for food and a cup of tea at homesteads along the road. Generally they met with sympathy and their immediate needs were supplied. It was a custom to cut some wood into suitable lengths for the stove or for the open hearth fire from the wood pile which was always somewhere near the kitchen door, while a cup of tea and food was being prepared by the cook or the lady of the house.

In later years, there were those who sought this food as their right and who resented giving any service in return because they regarded it as cheap labour, and occasionally I have seen cut wood carefully built over uncut wood to give the appearance of a large heap. There was also the hostess who gave rough service and unpalatable food. Fortunately such cases were few, and the accepted practice was carried out with good faith by seeker and giver. Sometimes a few shillings changed hands as well.

In the depths of the Depression, men were sometimes in no fit condition to cut wood or to give any arduous service in return, simply because they were weak from lack of sufficient food and were not physically fit for heavy or continuous work.

Sully was always willing to take a turn at the wood heap, and then appreciated the food supplied. He would not have a large pile of wood cut, but it was always well done and neatly stacked. A thank you in his soft voice accompanied by a friendly smile of appreciation in which his eyes took part mostly left the lady of the home well satisfied, and sometimes meant an extra gift for the road and maybe for the dog which had already shared his master's meal.

The Depression had made even such meals and small jobs difficult. Without work, it was no longer possible to keep up a reasonable appearance in clothes. This meant that Sully was not only in dire need, but felt he was not needed, not wanted, and that people and especially the police suspected him of being a good-for-nothing vagrant. He could do nothing to allay such suspicions, and through need was increasingly looking the part. Perhaps worst of all, he knew it.

Yet he fared better than most men on the road because he had learned through the years to live frugally – indeed a little flour for puftalooners or 'Johnny cakes' and a piece of mutton, lean or fat, supplied his wants. He liked to have tea and sugar too, but they were after all not a necessity. During the Depression, the New South Wales government had made a law granting those looking for work in country places a small ration worth about five shillings (fifty cents) a week. This was handed out each fortnight, and the police were in charge of its distribution. This handout was known as the dole and those without permanent home must be thirty miles away to be eligible for the next ration a fortnight later.

At this time, the early 1930s, the State Bank of New South Wales had been compelled to close its doors. Work was not available in Sydney, although a few received employment on the Harbour Bridge, which was in process of construction. In Sydney within my personal knowledge, families were turned out of homes for as little as £3 ($6) back rent. Some of these with other unemployed had left the city for the country in the hope of finding some sort of seasonal work. This hope was born of despair and seldom realised. These men mostly joined the numbers who had to keep moving to receive their fortnightly ration. I have seen men waiting round in the Riverina for weeks for a little harvest work at hay-cutting time, even staying in one place and missing a fortnightly ration, camping in old sheds or at showgrounds wherever a sort of shelter could be procured.

When at last work was offered, all too often because of the shortage of food, their strength was unequal to the constant heavy work and they were dismissed at the end of one or two days as incapable. Lack of experience in farm work often increased their disability. The work had to be done and done quickly, because in the event of a storm the farmer could easily lose the result of a year's work. He just dare not continue the employment of unfit or incompetent men.

Sometimes one heard of a government issue of clothes or boots to families in need, but the issue was never sufficient to meet the need, and the travelling man was of unknown character, and therefore unlikely to share in this inadequate issue.

In the country too, many were losing their homes where any mortgage was owing, and some were losing their farms because of the foreclosure of mortgages. Finally the government passed a moratorium law with regard to property, but large numbers by this time had nothing more to lose.

The dole or fortnightly ration, to the value of five shillings a week, did not supply sufficient food for the average man, even when he did not use any of it on smokes or drinks. It was also beset with many difficulties of collection, especially for the man with no settled home. To be thirty miles away for the next collection, and with no money to spend, presented grim situations such as sleeping under bridges, without means of keeping clean or tidy. It did at least preserve life, and in some cases prevent despair, robbery, breakdown or even suicide.

Many used to 'jump the rattler' – that is, ride on trains without tickets, sometimes in trucks or even finding a place beneath or above carriages – to travel the thirty miles so as to be eligible for the next fortnightly ration. Under these circumstances, an occasional tragedy was inevitable, and the police had instructions to prevent illegal train travel.

One evening in the Riverina, a police sergeant had been notified that many men were riding without tickets on an incoming train. Following this instruction, he met the train and arrested several men. Later at the police station where they were being charged, one, a Digger, threw down three war medals, a Military Medal, a Distinguished Conduct Medal and a Croix de Guerre, exclaiming in anger and despair, 'So this is what we bloody well fought for. They can have their bloody medals.' Such happenings reveal a little of the plight of many worthy men and the social and economic hopelessness of thousands of citizens, men and women too.

It was this economic breakdown that brought the carefree tramp with his few needs to the verge of despair. Because he had just collected his fortnightly ration at Mudgee, there was no sense of immediate anxiety in his mind over food. A further ration was due in a fortnight, and he knew how to conserve a meagre supply, so that there would be enough for him and his companion the dog. With clothes in tatters and boots turned up at the toes and without soles, he looked disreputable and was unlikely to get work even if it became available.

Of necessity, he had joined with scores of others who called at homes in search of work, and hoped at least to get a cup of tea and a few sandwiches for cutting wood or helping in some other way around the house or farm. Country people are kind, but as the banks closed on more and more homes, and others were refused credit to work their properties, it became harder for them to be kind in any way that cost money.

Laughingly, the tramp told me later how at this time he was camped at Wagga Wagga with a number of men and how on Monday morning they went to 'do the parsons'. The method was to call at the manse, parsonage or convent seeking work which was unlikely to be available, and then to ask for clothes and food. At the close of the morning, they met at their bridge camp to report and share the gifts.

As one of the parsons, I smiled too, because I had been done over a score of times at Coolamon, twenty-five miles north of Wagga Wagga. Some of these men had a gift of words, and not all of them were as honest or as truthful as our tramp. It was not uncommon in those days to give a cup of tea and something to eat to as many as six or eight men a day. Many are the stories of hope and hopelessness, of sickness and weakness, of resentment and bitterness that burnt themselves into my mind in a never to be forgotten manner, as these men called at our home and related some of their hardships.

Among many incidents, these two will never be erased from memory. The first, a young man of under twenty-one years, called for assistance, and while sandwiches were being cut and tea made, he was given a broom and asked to sweep a small hall, which would take about five minutes. On going to call him, he was found in a state of collapse and admitted that he had not eaten for almost two days.

The second incident was that of a lad about the same age who called for help. It was suggested that he go up to the wood heap while food was being prepared. He burst into abuse about cheap labour, and then told his story. He was dux of a large school around Newcastle and after leaving school was unable to obtain work. He had become bitter and swore that if ever he received work he would ruin the machines of the employer by 'sanding' them. His was understandable frustration. He did no work, but received a better meal than usual.

In the same decade, the Second World War came, and Australian manhood was needed and conscripted. For many young men, the war brought the first offer of a permanent job. Were these two lads among those who gave their lives for the land that made their first few years of manhood a hell of anxiety and suffering?

The tramp was so caught up in this same horror of unemployment that he needed a friend. Something must be done. To the everlasting credit of our police force, it was done. There was an old coach shed and stable at the back of our home that was still quite waterproof, and there the tramp found shelter and made his temporary home, which was to last several years. The police agreed to give him further rations at the station at Mudgee, while every effort was made to gain for him the age pension. Looking at the man with clothes so ragged, one could not help a feeling that he was genuine, and although something within also said, 'Don't be caught again, this is not your job,' something within also said, 'This man is genuine and in dire need. There's no one else to help him. Your position in the town makes it possible for you to help.'

He gladly took up residence in the stable building, part of which was in use as a garage, but the stable itself was not in use. It was about ten feet square, cobbled with rough stones, and with a feed box along one wall. The room was divided for two horses, and above was the one-time storage loft. At least it was dry shelter. After one look at it, his face relaxed as he quietly said, 'Thank you'. Then taking up the swag, he placed it inside and Paddy, the Border collie, sat beside it.

No one could be contacted who had known him for even one year. Never had he been out of New South Wales, but neither had he remained in any one place of recent years at least, long enough to be known. He was and always had been a tramp, a quiet, retiring tramp, who had little to say and kept to himself, but who through hard knocks in the ups and downs of life had developed an independent and determined personality all his own and quite unique.

At last the application for his pension was sent with no outside information or recommendation. It was sent in goodwill and with complete frankness. His birthplace was Redfern, Sydney. He believed it was just over sixty-five years ago. The application was accepted without undue delay, and within three months he was in receipt of the age pension with a sum of about £16 ($32) back money from the date of application. This was the greatest sum ever in his possession at one time, and his gratitude and pleasure at the pension, and his sheer elation on receiving back money, will never be forgotten.

He settled into the stable and established a garden and did small odd jobs, and as time went on grew and sold a few vegetables. The sight in his only eye was not good, so that he could only read large print. He would not miss church on Sunday, and really appreciated the friendliness of the congregation. This going to church was not because he was a churchgoing tramp, but out of deference to me. Seldom over the years had he felt tidy enough to mix with churchgoers, but on the rare occasions when an employer invited him to go, he made himself as tidy as possible and went, always sitting in the back seat. Now, after the purchase of a ready-made suit, he attended regularly. A few people always made sure to greet him with a cheerful word and these became his little circle of inner friends. One day in special confidence he said to me, 'I've always wanted to be a minister.' When small jobs came his way, he was a conscientious worker, but extremely slow and no doubt this accounted largely for his lack of success in making money out of land-clearing contracts.

Strangely enough, although he had little association with children through the years, he was very patient with them. He loved their company and enjoyed their chatter, and he in turn told them stories of his travels. His stories were never long because above all he was a man of few words. Our children often went to his room for a talk, and then up a perpendicular ladder, to the hay loft above which for years was their cubby house. They never worried about him being below and hearing their talk, and he was always pleased to have them about. Our boy, who at the time was about seven years old, was his special favourite. He called him 'little Kenny' and little Kenny always spoke of Mr Sully. I can hear Sully's chuckle and see the tears in his eyes as he told me proudly of something that Kenny had said or done. It made him happy to think that they had home care, which gave them security and an opportunity that he never had.

One day when Ken was on the loft, he moved out to the landing stage that twenty years before had been used for hauling up maize and chaff. There he stepped on the end of an unsuspected unnailed board that tilted him some ten or twelve feet to the ground. The doctor was called. Sully was greatly upset, and came several times that evening to ask how he was. Fortunately the boy escaped with a few scratches on his back, and a small amount of shock, but the kindness and anxiety of his old friend was touching to see.

During the time at Mudgee he made puftalooners every few weeks. 'Just to keep my hand in,' he would say, but really because he liked them so much. Occasionally our children saw him making them and went up to watch or, as they said, 'to help'. Perhaps the real reason was that they liked puftalooners too. After eating some, he would offer them one each, and to our surprise they were readily accepted and eaten with relish. I really believe they would have accepted a second had it been offered, but it never was.

There was another type of tramp well known to the people of inland towns as worthless fellows. Quite wrongly, many think of all tramps as belonging to this group. Tramps are not all of a type, and many a fine man has walked the roads because of tragedy of some sort in his early years. Sully had little in common with the all-too-prevalent drunkard type, or the metho drinker with trembling hands, or the sharper who would rather steal than work. These men seldom went far from cities and country towns, and lived by their wits, or perhaps I should say existed by their wits. The stories told by them, though untrue, were pathetic and well calculated to move the hearts of kindly people. These tramps, better called vagrants, tried very hard to get money or clothes without work. Occasionally they worked when really hard-up, but mostly the work was poorly done. If it happened to be gardening, weeds and flowers were treated indiscriminately. They would go to extremes to avoid work.

I well remember the man who agreed to roll a gravel croquet court and after a cup of tea and refreshments asked me to bring out the roller for him. I did so, and he thanked me nicely and asked just what I wanted done. After talking a few minutes, he said a spade would help him to scrape a few surface weeds. On returning in a few minutes with the spade, I found the roller just where I had placed it, but the man had gone.

Another called early in the morning and said he needed food and would work for it. He accepted the job offered, but hesitatingly broke the news that his wife was down the street and had nothing to eat. For her sake, would I advance him a couple of shillings on the job so that he could get her some breakfast. It would only take him a few minutes and it would mean so much to her. The money was advanced, but he did not return. At midday he was seen in the park, alone and drunk. He was a young methylated spirits drinker, and the suffering of such a one is great and his years few.

Another made a habit of calling every six months, and asked for odd jobs, but it was very little work that he ever did. This being known, he mostly received some sandwiches and perhaps a pair of socks, a shirt or some other clothing that he needed. He came at most awkward times and could be cheeky. One day coming at an inopportune time he further annoyed my wife by saying, 'I support all the churches. It makes no difference to me.' Yes, he supported all the churches, all the banks, all the doctors, and many other people and institutions by calling every three months for help. People pitied and often helped his kind, but did not respect them.

Shortly after Sully came, a tramp called late one afternoon and told a tale of hardship, lack of work, no money, and hunger. He wanted money to buy food, and he was cold and needed an overcoat. He was a man of about forty years of age, with trembling hands and bloodshot eyes that told their own tale of methylated spirits and instability. He received an overcoat and a parcel of food, but he appeared disappointed at not receiving money. Sully watched all this unknown to me, and when the man left, he followed him to his camp, which was under the bridge at the entrance to the town. A number of other men were there. Sully joined them and talked as a fellow tramp. He heard the man tell the others that I was no good for money, but that he did get food. He also boasted that he put it over me about clothes, and had received a good overcoat that he would sell the next day for quite a bit of cash. Later Sully left them. The next morning he came and reproved me for being so easily taken in, saying, 'He was a metho drinker and not worth helping, but I didn't like to interfere. I followed him to the camp and there he was boasting to others of how he put it over you, and proved it by showing them the good overcoat he was going to sell the next day.' This was the only time he reproved me, but I had helped him and it hurt him to see me apparently taken in.

During this period, an appointment was made with the Sydney Dental Clinic. With frugal living and the back pension money, he was well-off even after the purchase of a cheap new Sunday suit. He returned from Sydney set up with a complete set of teeth – his own, with the exception of two, had long since departed. He was proud of this first set of dentures, always wearing them on special occasions, but regularly taking them out to eat.

While in Sydney, he stayed somewhere in Redfern, but was not able to make contact in any way with his life there as a boy. This disappointed him, because he had always believed that he could find the house where his early and unhappy years were spent, and around which still lingered thoughts of a mother who had sought to protect him, and was often herself abused and in dire need. He stayed at a residential hostel, but could not give any idea of the street or direction from the railway. He could have returned to it unerringly, but this man who knew thousands of miles of road in New South Wales had not developed the same sense of street names or numbers in cities.

The lack of city sense was again demonstrated on a journey to Orange some twelve months later. Again the trip was taken by rail and he found a place to board for a few days. After his return, we were talking over his experiences when suddenly he put his hand to his mouth and said, 'Good Lord, my teeth!' I anxiously enquired what was wrong with them, and he replied, 'They're under the pillow at Orange.' Having placed them under the pillow for safety because he preferred to sleep and eat without them, they were completely forgotten until that moment. On enquiry, he could remember going up the street from the railway and taking a left turn and a right turn and another left turn, but did not know the name of the street or of the boarding house. He said, 'I could find it if I went back,' but he did not want to go back again. We advertised in hope but with no result, and he remained without teeth. Having always taken them out to eat, he did not find the loss so great.

A new phase of his character was seen and things were suddenly changed by his dog, Paddy. A neighbour's girl, about four years old, often came into the large backyard. This day, she went up to the old stable, saw the dog tied up, and as he sat quivering with excitement because of her presence, she poked her little face within a few inches of his and stared at him. Suddenly he snapped, and blood appeared under one eye and on the cheek below. She ran home crying, and her mother rang for the doctor. No real damage was done. They complained to me, and were much distressed at the time. Later that day, I told the tramp he would have to get rid of the dog. He just looked at me, and after a pause said quietly without a sign of anger, but rather sadly, 'Well, if the dog must go, I'll go too.'

At the time, I did not treat his remark seriously, thinking that in a day or two we could talk it over, and reach a compromise. The very next morning the shed was empty. Both he and the dog had gone. They had left probably at the break of day and before sunrise.

For more than a year, he resumed the tramp's life and we never heard a word. Then one day he returned and took up residence, but he was alone. He did not wish to speak of Paddy, but from a word dropped some time later, it appeared that he died after being struck by a motor car.

From that time on, he never lost touch with us. When we moved to another country town, he moved too and, being affluent now, he purchased a tent and lived beside a creek half a mile away. There again he made just a few friends who knew of his camp and liked the little old quiet and honest man.

Later when we moved to Sydney, the problem was greater. But he came and looked around, and then settled in a small ten feet by six feet tin shack with a chimney that he found deserted in the bush about two miles south east of Windsor. Later I visited him there.

Finally at seventy-four years of age, he accepted an offer to live in the Home for Aged People in Windsor. There he was very happy. It was at that home that, as far as I could ever discover, he had his first thoughts of marriage. One of the old ladies was very kind to him, and telling me about it, he said, 'They say I'll be marrying her.' He blushed like a boy while telling me. I think he enjoyed the thought, as he appreciated the kindness of the woman, but this man of the open spaces was such a confirmed bachelor that he could never bring himself to taking a wife.

At one stage, the home rang me to say he had gone bush with a swag, although seventy-six years of age. Both the matron and the secretary of the home liked him and were anxious for his welfare. After nearly three months, he returned. Truly the Australian bush was now in the blood of the one-time little Redfern boy.

This was his last walkabout. He returned to the home, and six months later, one morning, they found him dead in bed. Maybe his spirit had gone for another walkabout and did not wish to return. I am certain this is how he would have desired it.

The report came to me in this letter:

Windsor Home of Aged

Dear...
    I regret to inform you that Mr Alfred James Sully passed away in his sleep yesterday.
    He received a public funeral this morning.
    Yours faithfully,
    ....
    Sec. Windsor Home for Aged.

It would have been a great privilege to conduct, or even attend, that funeral.

In the simple things of everyday life, he was great. No one in any sphere of activity had been more faithful than he in his.

Sully as an old man in his new Sunday suit with Paddy

The Parson

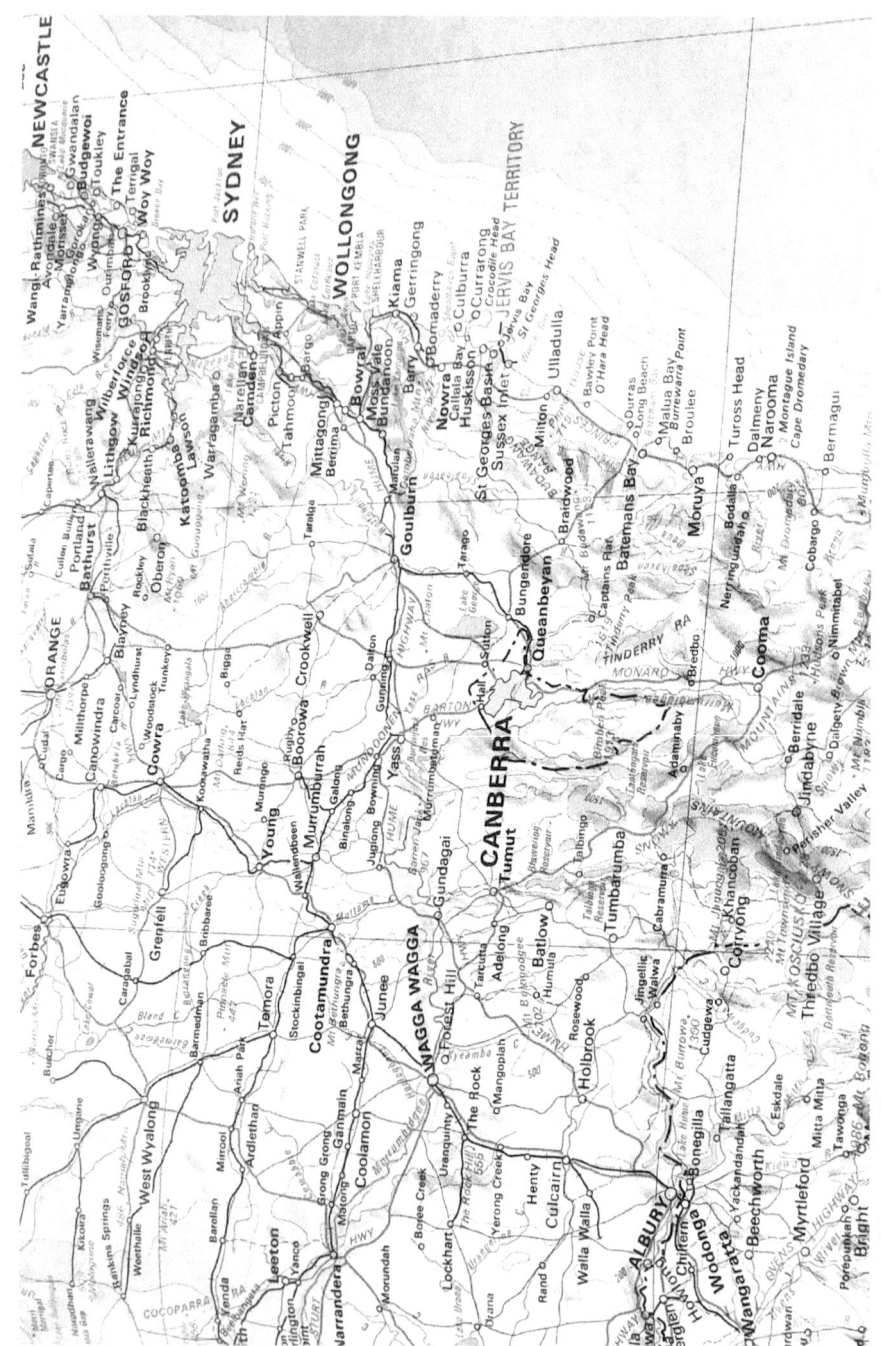

Introduction

In 1925, Rev. Russell French Gibson LTh (RFG as he initialled documents) married Miss Enid Muriel Shield BA, a recent graduate from the University of Sydney. She was twenty-five and he twenty-eight. Born in 1900, Muriel, as she was known, had been appointed to the new high school at Cooma. There she had attended the Methodist church and met the new minister. RFG had obtained his Licentiate in Theology just two years previously. Cooma and Bombala were his first independent churches as a minister of religion.

Marriage of Rev. and Mrs R.F. Gibson, Leichardt, 1925

Their first daughter was born in 1926. Soon there was another daughter and then a son. I was their last child, born over twenty years after my eldest sister. A baby boomer, I am really two generations apart from my father, who was over fifty at the time of my birth. My two sisters and one brother were almost a generation apart from me too. I grew up with my nieces and nephews.

Because I was not there for any part of the original story of Sully the Swagman, or the family's life in country NSW, I went on a journey to find out more.

Arts graduates, University of Sydney, 1920; Muriel Shield front row, 6th from left

1

My travels begin

On a wet, windy, southern Tasmania afternoon in winter, I set out. It takes over five hours to reach Devonport on the north coast. The whole way, my windscreen wipers twitch and squeak but at least the heater keeps my feet warm. For a few hours, I try to nap in the back seat of 'Ashoka-3', my Toyota Camry. It doesn't work and never again on this journey will I try squeezing in and out this way. I feel like a wombat emerging rump-first from a tight burrow.

Before 6 a.m., bleary-eyed and expectant, I queue to manoeuvre my vehicle into the bowels of the *Spirit of Tasmania*. Gale-force winds and rough seas have delayed the ship's return journey from Melbourne by several hours. Now it has to be unloaded and cleaned before receiving its new load of vehicles and passengers. My parents had made a similar journey, late in life, from NSW to Tasmania. Launceston was their fifteenth posting in a long ministry.

We wait. It's past midday when, with a long and triumphal blast of the horn, the *Spirit* finally pulls out from the dock to negotiate the seas between northern Tasmania and the mainland, or, as Tasmanians say, 'the big island'. We head directly into Bass Strait.

Until 1798, European explorers did not know that Van Diemen's Land (now Tasmania) was an island, separated from the mainland of Australia by the sea's rise ten thousand years before. Though Cook (our distant relative), and later Bligh and the French navigators had explored the coastline, it remained to Matthew Flinders and his companion George Bass to demonstrate finally that such a strait did exist.

Strong currents between the Antarctic (south-east) part of the Indian Ocean and the Pacific Ocean waters of the Tasman Sea make for a strait with powerful and wild storms. Twice the width of the English Channel and twice as rough, the number of ships wrecked on the Tasmanian and Victorian coastlines number in the hundreds. Many vessels have disappeared without a trace. Stories of piracy and supernatural phenomena like the Bermuda Triangle abound. Really, these disappearances are the result of treacherous wind and sea conditions and semi-submerged rocks. In spite of these difficult waters, since 1800 Bass Strait has provided a safer passage for ships from Europe or India en route to Sydney, It also cut 1,300 kilometres off the distance. The first settlement outside Sydney occurred in Hobart in 1803 to forestall any French claims and, later, anticipated Russian warships.

Although I know the *Spirit of Tasmania* is not about to founder today, waves crash against the reinforced windows till I fear they will crack and let water gush in. The vessel is frequently raised tens of metres by huge waves, only to crash down again with the troughs. Captain and crew have to reduce speed. We passengers sit nauseous and listless, not daring to eat. Some carry tightly closed seasick bags to rubbish bins.

Sully would never have encountered this turbulence – his vessel was stationary. The thought of his life on board makes me shudder, though. It would have been claustrophobic for one thing – and that probably not the worst of it. My father too was a poor sailor, though he loved fishing (until he became a vegetarian late in life). Even the gentle rocking of a boat could make him ill. He hadn't fared well on his crossings of Bass Strait.

Eventually we reach the shelter of the enclosed Port Phillip Bay an hour or so before docking in Melbourne. Everyone comes back to life. The ship's cafés are busy. When we disembark in the dark, I become lost in the crazy paving of inner Melbourne's port and city roads. It's midnight before I reach my destination. What does all this mean, if anything, for the rest of my adventure?

After spending a week with my daughter and grandchildren, I've recovered from the nightmare crossing. Now I'm eager to set off in search of Sully the Swagman and my father, Russell Gibson. Leaving early on another wet, wintry Saturday morning, I follow the Hume Highway out of Melbourne without a hitch – thanks to my daughter's directions. When I reach Seymour, it's still bleak and grey but not wet.

Parked in the main street, I stroll past shops beside the railway and read a sign. This of course is Station Street. How many station streets there must be in the English-speaking world? Seymour services a mainly agricultural area. Since 1872 it has been a significant stop on the railway line between Melbourne and Albury on the NSW border to the north-east. Around 1880, a branch line headed north to Shepparton and so will I. Seymour is the hometown of the nearby army base, Puckapunyal, some ten kilometres west. A restricted military establishment, it was first used as a mobilisation and training area during World War I. Though I've often heard the name, a rendering of an indigenous Australia name, until today I'd no clear idea of its location.

My father had not actually served in World War I, though he was of age. Because I was born after World War II, I had little knowledge or interest in warfare. As a university student, I had vehemently opposed the Vietnam War, being recorded in a photograph on the front page of a left-wing publication. Unlike much of the world, I'd been fortunate enough, so far, not to have had to take much notice of military matters. My father's life required a decision between the army and the church. These two possibilities circled his early years until a combination of circumstances helped decide his future course.

Pleased to have learnt where Puckapunyal is, I find my way onto the Goulburn Valley Highway, the A39. I pass through Shepparton, except for a fuel stop, and head north towards little-known places – towns whose names have been family memories, mentioned around the Christmas dinner table, on family birthdays or picnics, whenever my parents and older sibling gathered. Following the straight system of grid-like roads displayed on my map, I cross the Murray River and drift into NSW. It's such an insignificant border that it all seems an anticlimax today.

I find myself in Tocumwal. Umbrella in one hand against the drizzle,

I climb a grassy levee bank to gaze into the Murray's clouded waters. Dotted with occasional shady eucalypts, the embankment is set up as foreshore parkland. I imagine that on fine days it must be a wonderful area for picnicking and fishing. This feels like a milestone – I am now in the country of Sully the Swagman and my younger parents.

Tocumwal in the Berrigan Shire is said to be named for the local word meaning 'a deep hole in the river'. It was, so I learnt, the place where the largest Murray cod was caught. First settled by pastoralists in the 1840s, it was, before Federation, an important customs point for goods crossing between the colonies of Victoria and New South Wales. Many of these south-western Riverina towns were unhappy that they had been included in NSW rather than Victoria. Their citizens were, before 1901, some of the strongest supporters for a federation of Australian states.

In the 1850s, a decade or so before Sully's birth, the new colony of Victoria was separated from NSW, the district of Port Phillip being declared Victoria on 1 July 1851. The borders between Victoria, NSW and SA have generated more litigation than any others. The western border of what was originally all NSW and SA was marked by the 141 meridian. The lower part of this became the border with Victoria, while the Murray River defined the northern boundary of Victoria (and the southern one of NSW). But which bank was the border, or should it be the middle of the river?

In 1980, the High Court in *Ward v R* established the precise boundary between NSW and Victoria along the River Murray as the top of the southern bank of the river. At this time, the court interpreted s5 of the *Constitution Act 1855 (Imperial)* which had deemed the whole watercourse of the River Murray to be in NSW – encompassing the top of one bank to the top of the other. Ward had fired a shot from the top of the southern bank of the Murray River, the Victorian side, which had killed a man on the other shore of the river, in NSW. According to this decision, the offence was committed in NSW and not in Victoria. Of course it was not the first time state boundaries had played an important role in Australia's judicial history. Ned Kelly and his gang used them regularly to escape the police, whose colonial authority ended at the state boundary.

At Tocumwal, I pore over the maps in my giant *Atlas of Australia*. Once across the border, the Goulburn Valley Highway becomes the Newell Highway, while retaining its status as the A39. A large wire spiral in the centre between the two pages obscures the town names I want. I decide to continue twenty-one kilometres north to Finley, a nondescript town with large wheat silos. They look much as they had in my father's old photograph. Deserting the Newell Highway, I turn east onto the flat Riverina Highway. It runs beside an old canal built to service local agricultural land. It's another ordinary inland road with a dotted median line, apart from the narrower bridges. I am heading for Berrigan.

Berrigan's a vaguely familiar name from my family's history. A name from a very early time in my father's life when he was first ordained a minister. As a young man, he'd broken his leg near Berrigan. And that was why, fifty years later, he strongly – and I do mean strongly – discouraged me from ever riding a motorbike. Not ever…even when I thought of driving through Asia and on into Europe in the early 1970s. How I wish now that I had. All those lands of present suffering and unfailing misery were open then. Besides, I had a great English companion, a school friend who had lived there, Agatha Christie style, as a child. So Berrigan had a bearing on my own life too – a bike trip I did not take.

As I delve back now into some faded small photographs crying out for restoration, I find one I'd overlooked. It's a dark, overexposed mass with a horse's head and a man's head, standing out before the lighter skyline. Turning it over, I read my father's neat, careful handwriting, so unlike my mother's looped carelessness and my own untidy scrawl. He has chosen to write his missive diagonally across the black and white print which he must have developed himself: 'The Berrigan parson and turn out; this photo is somewhat over-developed but will give you an idea of the circuit outfit taken 21/7/'23'.

When I peer closely, I see the typical clergyman's white clerical collar above the darkness of his other attire. I assume that a 'turn out' is a horse and trap, a cart on which RFG would sit to drive. It would also carry his accoutrements as he travelled. Sometimes he had to cover many, many miles

The Berrigan parson

between churches. Methodist circuits – what the Anglican Church often termed a parish – always had more than one country church to serve as well as many parishioners who did not live in town. Who was this photo sent to? He had not married in 1923 so I expect it was to his beloved mother.

John Gibson had married Mary Jane, the youngest daughter of a nearby Dapto farmer, James Griffin. An upright Englishman from the Home Counties, James had played the cornet at Queen Victoria's coronation before migrating to NSW as a paying passenger in the 1850s. Mary Jane and John Gibson had two sons, the elder Victor and the younger Russell French Gibson. My father told me long afterwards that John Gibson was not his mother's first love. She was over thirty when her sons were born – unusual for those days, I would have thought. I have never been able to unravel why the marriage

Mary Jane Gibson, RFG's mother, Murwillumbah, c. 1917

caused John's father, Edward Gibson, to disinherit him in favour of his two younger sons.

Left with no property of their own, the family soon migrated north. Their dairy cattle were transported by sea on an iron paddle steamer; originally a two-mast schooner from Glasgow named the *City of Grafton*. Owned by the North Coast Steam Navigation Company, Sydney, it plied the coastal ports trade routes, including the Clarence River. The family purchased farming land around Clunes near Lismore. A few years later, John Gibson sold stock and land at a profit and moved the family further north to Murwillumbah on the border of Queensland. They remained there at 'Tweed View' till John's death.

'Tweed View', the Gibsons' dairy farm, Murwillumbah, northern NSW, c. 1915

Mary Jane Gibson (my paternal grandmother) died sometime in the 1940s, well before my birth. Her husband, John, had died much earlier and very suddenly in 1915. It was to change RFG's life. His teenage diary records,

> March 14, Sunday, 1915, I started to teach Sunday school today. Got along very well…
>
> Father died suddenly this evening, about 4 o'clock heart-failure. He had not been ailing very much though often had complained of pain over the heart, he was very ill on Saturday night (though fairly well on Saturday & went to town, also had a good tea) had no sleep & I heard him say he never had such a bad night in his life. He would not go to a doctor on Sunday as he always disliked going near a doctor, but did not dress; just lying about on veranda & sofa. He had been retching during night & day. The pain started in the left arm or hand, went up the arm & lodged over heart; it was during

one of these attacks of retching that father passed-away. I am so thankful that in our trouble I feel that God is ever nigh, ever with me, with us & I am quite content to know that he is with us to trust him, to leave my feet sure in His hands.

Speaking onto tape many years later, RFG recalled the same incident somewhat differently.

My father was planning to go for a holiday back to his own place Dapto. He and mother had set the date, two or three months ahead. If they'd gone and come back, I would have gone to the war. Father wouldn't have stopped me. He wouldn't have fought me over it at any rate and I'd made my mind up that's what I'd do. Stay and help keep the farm going while they were away – we had to run it and then I'd go when he came back. But he never got away.

He died like that in one day. He went for a long ride on the Saturday for miles and miles on his old horse… He came home and he wasn't too well on Sunday, he was out on our veranda. We had a very nice veranda it was all marble slabs, square and it was very pretty in a way. And he used to go out there very often, he had a chair he'd sit on. This day he was out there and he went to lie down on the slabs and I heard a peculiar noise and I went out, he was unconscious. He'd been coughing and I know what it was because I saw black, I looked and he had two black spots on his neck.

The artery had broken there at the back of his neck near the vertebrae, just above that big one. I could see the two black spots when he was lying down. He'd coughed and that evidently broke the artery. I'm sure he was conscious when I went out to him but he couldn't speak. I helped to sit him up. I don't know if that was wise or not, perhaps not. I don't think it made any difference. I think he was gone. But his eyes were quite clear and I knew he was conscious but he couldn't speak or say anything. He died within seconds or within a minute or two at any rate, while I was supporting him.

Vic rode in for the doctor. He had 5 miles to ride and he galloped all the way and the doctor came out. It was before the days of cars I think. He came out on a horse. He had a car soon after that but I don't think he had a car then. He didn't when my father died because there were not cars about much. He just told us father had passed away and he went away again.

But that was the final straw about my enlisting for the war. I couldn't go then that's why I blame my Mother, she wouldn't let me. Before he died I hadn't said anything to either of them because I was keeping quiet until they had the holiday. He wouldn't have stopped me.

On 29 July 1914, RFG attended his first Light Horse parade. An earnest young man at the time, he wrote,

> They are the foulest minded fellows in ALH [Australian Light Horse] that I ever met, practically all.

Then, just a few days later he records,

> August 4th 'England declared war on Germany at 12 o'clock to night (day time in England). This war has been forced upon England may God watch over her.

Even after his father's death, RFG's church activities and his military training – the two strands of his life – continued throughout 1915.

> I went to camp on Thursday 8th [April] arrived back on 16th with a fresh cold. Received a letter from Edie [RFG's cousin] before I went (Tues) which settled any doubts I had on what I should do. Camp was certainly profane & immoral to a surprisingly large extent. But they allowed me to go my way (reading my bible and praying every night) without molestation.

Enlisting for the war was still on his mind, however:

> July 15th 1915 … Heard to day that George Brooks & Arthur Mansbridge are going to the war. I feel that my place is now there also, if I can pass. Mother says I cannot go; but am in hopes that she will alter that decision.

My father's mother did not reverse her decision and by September he was very much involved in church study and planning sermons. In 1982 RFG recalled,

> I wanted to go to the war because I thought I should. Well I was in the Light Horse at the time and that was a bad point for staying home. I was in the cadets at school. As soon as I was old enough to get out of the cadets, 17 probably, I went to several [Australian Imperial Forces, AIF] camps. I was a very religious chap when I went to the camps I got into trouble with some of the boys for I would say my prayers at nights. I saw quite a few lots of boots. Some of them were pretty rough types. They all were pretty rough types really.
>
> But there was one chap I liked all right but he was the roughest type of the lot. He was a real rough chap and he took my side. He told some of those

chaps, 'if I see you do anything.' I suppose he called me with Russ Gibson, 'if I see you doing anything with him again, you'll have me to deal with.' It stopped. I always respected him at any rate. He was a decent chap and he meant it too. They weren't game to throw any more boots.

And by the way, the sergeant major came very quietly one day and he said he appreciated what I was doing which was rather good because he was fairly rough too. A lot of our sergeant majors were queer chaps. They could swear like anything. In fact they all did like swearing, putting it over the boys or showing off to the boys. That's why when he came to me with a word of congratulations, of appreciation, well I began to think he was a decent sort… and probably he was in his own way but they liked to swear and tell dirty yarns so that they were all right with the boys. I had to put up with that sort of thing because it was the natural life with those chaps. Vic joined the cadets and he went into the footsloggers – Infantry. It hurt me very much not going to the war. I wanted to whether or not. Vic never really wanted to. Mother took the firm stance she wouldn't let me go at any rate. I was old enough I was 18 but I had to have my parents' consent.

Having begun to teach at Sunday school the previous year, Russ Gibson now prepared and gave his first practise sermons under supervision. He wrote,

May 10th
Had our first meeting at Mr Somerville's to help us toward preaching the Gospel: Alf George & myself. God was with us as I know He will ever be.
Went again to camp from 12th to 16th.

As his possibility of enlisting faded, his calling to the ministry became stronger.

Strange how these things are still in my memory now, after nearly 80 years. I felt that I had a call to the ministry. I felt that I had to. It was a type of vision or something of that type. I just felt I had to do it. And because of that I just did it. I wouldn't do anything else. … It came in various ways.

One day when I was reading the bible, a text stood out. It stood out in huge letters. It was distinct from anything else I'd ever seen or heard. It said, 'let the dead bury their dead,' and by then it was early war time. And I was trying to go and Mother wouldn't let me.

It stood out, 'Let the dead bury their dead, but go thou and preach the kingdom of God.' To me it was as clear as anything could be. And that definitely made up my mind. I was 17 or 18, I think 18 but it settled me then. I felt I had to do that and nothing else and that settled the whole thing.

Mary Jane Gibson with her sons Russell (left) and Victor, c. 1916

Tocumwal, Finlay and Berrigan were all part of the same circuit which, for a short time, RFG ran in the early 1920s. Though young, unmarried and untried, he was a fully ordained Methodist clergyman. The farm boy had become the Reverend R.F. Gibson LTh.

Group of trainee ministers, Leigh College, Sydney, 1920; RFG centre front

2

Bikes and breaks

Everywhere I drive is flat. The swagman and my father had known this area intimately. I hadn't grasped its unending uniformity till now. The weather in Berrigan, like all the towns I've stopped in today, is dull with intermittent splashes of rain. 'Overcast' was the word my father always used to describe such weather. It's hard to imagine how hot these places are in summer. How must it have been for someone tramping or riding these roads a hundred years earlier when they were all dirt?

Because of Berrigan's location near the Victorian border it was one of the keenest to push for Australian federation. Like other small border towns that found themselves in NSW, it would have preferred to be with Victoria. Locals were anxious to abolish the border customs posts that involved added expenses carting produce to Melbourne and the south.

The Berrigan post office opened in 1884. Today the town has an ageing population apart from the few young ones I met. In 2013, an Alzheimer's wing was opened to service this farming district.

Thirsty and hungry, I pull up beside the local takeaway shop. All the way it has been too wet to try my gas burner or use the food supplies in the boot. As I step out, avoiding the running water, I'm relieved to find it open. My last food was at Seymour, a long time ago. Outside on a plastic chair beside the variegated fly strips hanging across the open door sits a young lad. I guess he is waiting for his takeaway until his voice greets me unexpectedly and I realise he's in charge of the shop.

I wait for my hamburger. It is the first and will be possibly the best I'll have this road trip. He prepares me a cup of tea – my favourite Earl

Grey, no less. I notice him pull back in pain trying not to call out as the boiling water spills onto his hand. He's using the boiling tap attached to the coffee machine. I begin to worry about his survival. How many cups of tea has he made before? A large bright cup with a bowl on top, full of sugar and milk sachets, soon appears. My appreciation is very real as I sip this death-defying cuppa.

Would I like onion on my burger? Yes, please. Egg? No, thank you. Beetroot? Certainly. Would you want pineapple? We both nod agreement. Pineapple as well does seem a bit much. It's a culinary enterprise, this hamburger. Eventually it arrives at my table, complete with tomato sauce. It makes a very substantial meal. The young man hovers. I am his only customer. He returns from time to time to see if it needs more sauce. Does it meet with my approval? I assure him it does.

Several women return to the shop as I munch. They chat behind the counter. An extraordinarily large young woman enters to order a takeaway. She's the only other customer I see. Before leaving with his mother, possibly the shop's proprietor, the lad bids me a warm goodbye. Loudly, in front of everyone, I announce what a grand hamburger maker he is. Perhaps it's the first he has ever made alone. His friendly eagerness to please lifts a grey day for this solitary traveller.

Weather makes such a difference. If it were sunny, I would walk. Now, because it is about to rain again, I drive unenthusiastically around the small and anything but booming town. What was it like in 1922/23? The past still lingers in Berrigan, more than in a busier place. Probably my father's Methodist church would have been replaced. Anyway I can't find it.

Two brothers John and Charles Wesley while at Oxford were the principal founders of the 'method-ist' movement in eighteenth century England. Both were ordained Anglican ministers, as was their father. They developed strong reformist and social justice components to their preaching. Charles was a great hymn writer and many of his verses are still used today by various denominations. Those hymns were my first introduction to poetry.

Methodism appealed to working people as well as the establishment and was influential in the abolishment of slavery. In Wales their churches were known as 'chapels' but not in NSW. Curiously both my parents' families had Anglican connections and they both became Methodists almost by chance. In Australia the Methodists were one organisation with separate state administrations – from 1902until 1977.

In 1977 the Methodist Church of Australasia, of which my father was a minister, merged to form a new church – The Uniting Church in Australia. It joined the Congregational Union of Australia and half of the Presbyterian Church of Australia. (Other Presbyterians decided to keep their own identity and property.) Today there is no original Methodist church in Australia, just as there are no more swagmen.

With a combination of the three churches, each town and suburb in Australia usually found two churches 'surplus to requirements'. They, and their parsonages or manses, were gradually sold off or used for other purposes. Mostly the better church building became the Uniting Church with its new symbol – the red dove on white cross with black background.

If I was eager (I was always brightest in the mornings), I'd walk around these churches, look for a dedication stone, or any other indication as to what breed of church it had once been. If I came across the name Wesley, for instance, it was a sure sign the church had been a Methodist one. Once a church had been sold, it might become anything – a shop, a home, a school, a restaurant or a night club.

Travelling on, I found various interesting resurrected churches and some surprises. Often too I had a chuckle at myself and the absurdity of what I was doing. Who else would be searching for old Methodist churches?

At Berrigan in the very early 1920s, before he met the tramp, the young RFG decided to try a powerful motorbike as alternative transport to the turn out and horse for his church work. This photo must have been taken somewhere in the town. The sheds look old, even then.

It was a Harley-Davidson that rolled on my father's leg breaking it and leaving him, trapped beneath it, alone and unattended on a country road all night until sometime the next morning. Later he learnt the frame was broken and patched in four places. On his recovery, the church bought

RFG and his motorbike, Berrigan, 1923

him a new motorbike which gave no trouble. I know this part of his life in Berrigan was before the time he met the swagman – by then he was driving a car.

It is no wonder RFG never forgot this accident. All his life he kept a reply from his lecturer to the letter he must have sent describing his accident. RFG had completed all the requirements for a Doctor of Divinity but because he was not encouraged to complete a BA degree he was instead awarded a Licentiate in Theology (LTh). He was an excellent scholar of Greek and Hebrew and would very much have liked to have continued academically. However, his church required practical working ministers.

No doubt RFG was some considerable time off full work, recovering. As far as I know, he was never troubled by the broken leg again but it must have left him sympathetic to any lone traveller, such as Sully, he might come across.

I head back to Finlay along the same flat irrigation canal-side road to rejoin the Newell Highway and continue north-east to the city of Narrandera. The only town of note I pass is Jerilderie, but I am not a

Wesley College, University of Sydney

Newtown,
4 June 1922

Dear Mr Gibson,
I write to thank you for your letter of 26th May & also to express our sympathy with you. A knowledge of Greek, does not (evidently) help you to master a motorcycle on a slippery road. Just as well to know the learn limitations of human knowledge — even in so excellent a subject as Hellenistic!

However, let me say how very sorry we were to hear of your accident & we hope that you are now making a good recovery.

It will be cold in your neighbourhood. Last week I was at Blackheath for a few days with Mrs Scott Fletcher & we found it quite bitter. Among the snows of the Southern Alps you must find it quite good to have a valid excuse to remain in bed — where I picture you.

With every good wish,
Yours sincerely,
Jn Scott Fletcher.

My warmest congratulations on your success in the diploma examinations — go on!

Letter from RFG's lecturer

Ned Kelly pilgrim today and winter dark is closing in. Ned too used the Murray River border to nip across into NSW whenever he was pursued by Victorian state police.

The afternoon's gigantic hamburger, supplied with fresh hot chips, unasked for – one of my uncontrollable favourites – means I'm not hungry. A supply of nibbles including dry fruit and nuts keeps me happy for the rest of the day as I push on.

It is very dark when I drive into Narrandera past a huge pit-stop garage lit up like a mining town. Parked around it, there seem to be hundreds of huge road vehicles about to travel west across the Hay Plains to South Australia or returning. Many campervans too have pulled in there for the night. Maybe I should too but I continue into the town.

Though I need a rest, I'm too tired to seek out accommodation in the dark and wet. Turning off the main road, I pull up beside a nursing home. Sheltered by a leafy roadside tree, I gather my blankets from the rear and a couple of pillows for my back and head. Releasing the lever, I let the seat back as far as I can and fall asleep.

I don't wake till just before dawn, around 5 a.m. Though my neck is a little sore, I feel remarkably refreshed and starving hungry. Backtracking across the Murrumbidgee River bridge, I enter the roadhouse. It's open twenty-four hours and I'm one of the first morning customers. Though there are showers in the ladies' toilets, I can't quite face one so early in the day. It is very cold. I will stop early in the evening and find somewhere comfortable. But it is good to clean my teeth.

I begin to wonder about Sully. How did he clean his teeth (in the early days when he had some)? Were toothbrushes available or did he, like so many I'd known in India, prefer a fresh scented twig from a local tree? Since early childhood I'd loved the smell of eucalyptus and had been known to crunch on gum nuts. In India, the neem tree was usually the preferred choice for dental care. But our eucalypts have much to recommend them. My father used eucalyptus oil for many things and probably Sully did too. Did he, like my mother, have false teeth early – or no teeth before his later dentures?

Along with Vicks (rubbed on the chest), eucalyptus oil was always dabbed on my pyjamas when I had a cold. RFG would also put a drop in his mouth. Eucalyptus oil or Dettol (my mother's choice), was also good to cleanse small cuts and abrasions – its sting a guarantee that it was killing germs. Family health patterns are absorbed so early that they are often unrecognised. Like dietary habits.

Replete with several cups of tea, a substantial roadhouse breakfast and clean teeth, I wander the broad, imposing main street of Narrandera. Like most Riverina towns, the main street is very wide. Perhaps it was the turning circle for a horse and dray. I pass a large, imposing NAB bank building, a two storey residence. Peering more closely, I see it was originally the Commercial Banking Company of Sydney, a bank first established in 1834, with this Narrandera branch following in 1880. A friend of mine born and raised around Narrandera is the only other person I know of who remembers this bank. My father knew it very well. In the early days, it was a significant feature of the Riverina. Later in the 1970s or 1980s, it merged to form NAB, the National Australia Bank, one of the current big four Australian banks. Before its rebranding, Westpac had been the Bank of NSW. ANZ of course always had trans-Tasman links, while the Commonwealth Bank – the child of Ben Chifley and post-war Labor – had Commonwealth government links. It was the red tape and lack of flexibility in its procedures that caused RFG at least once to move church finances to the more accommodating CBC bank.

Just twenty-two kilometres east of Narrandera, I reach Grong Grong, a strange, flat, dismal little place. Here the Newell Highway continues north. The map tells me it is here I divert east for Coolamon. I want to locate the hot and dusty road between Ganmain and Coolamon where the parson first encountered the tramp. To do so, I will have to turn off again onto a narrower, unmarked bitumen road. A century has made improvements here too. It is no longer a dusty dirt track and certainly not hot at this time of year. But it's where RFG first met Sully.

3

Ganmain & Coolamon

The second of August 2015 is again a gloomy wintry day. There are no clouds to be seen apart from a fleck on the horizon.

Grong Grong derives its name from an Aboriginal word meaning 'bad camping place', so the sign informs. I find myself laughing out loud. Why would anywhere want to admit this? The location isn't appealing yet the town has done its best to be welcoming. I manage to fit behind the inward-opening female toilet door, while avoiding the toilet bowl. It's squeezed closely beside the male one and inside is scarcely big enough for a moderate-sized woman to perch. Again more drizzle prevents me brewing a cup of tea in the tiny picnic shed.

The Ganmain–Coolamon road, 2015

I head off along the road to Coolamon. It's tarred and has that broken white line in the centre. Over ninety years ago, my father first met the swagman somewhere here. I try to imagine it then in wet weather, a rutted track hugging the railway line from Narrandera to Coolamon. Both roadway and rail line are built up slightly on embankments, raised above the flat surrounding countryside. It must have been the same in Sully's day. Scattered gum trees accept the drizzly day as they do everything else, without complaint. It's eight degrees now. I'm told this country can have heavy frost too, in winter. But it must have been very hot tramping on dirt roads here in the summer.

I am in a time warp. This part of NSW seems scarcely to have changed. Few cars come along the flat, straight road. At regular intervals, dirt roads branch off the bitumen at right angles. Private access for the various farming properties, I guess. Though trees are scattered irregularly over the landscape, it's pleasant country. I imagine Sully would have walked, sat, or trudged along here. Perhaps I'll see him in a moment.

This will be the busiest, fullest day of my journey to retrace the steps of the Swagman, my Methodist parents and older siblings. On my large motoring atlas, the Ganmain Road is scarcely any distance off the slightly wider road to Coolamon. I stop to take photos of the flat, repetitive scenery. I am beginning to understand what the Riverina is all about.

The Riverina is a descriptive term used regularly in the tramp's tale by my father. It is a rich, agricultural region in the west and south of NSW, distinguished by flat plains and a warm to hot climate. But not today. It has plentiful water or easy irrigation from the roadside canals. I'd followed some en route to Berrigan yesterday and I am seeing more of them again today. With Victoria to the south, to the east lies the Great Dividing Range, making the Riverina one of the most productive and agriculturally diverse areas of Australia. Not only the Murray but also the Murrumbidgee River supplies it with water. It is part of the larger Murray–Darling basin and most streams and rivers in the Riverina flow east to west. Rain falls mostly in winter, which explains what I've experienced yesterday and today.

The Wiradjuri peoples have inhabited the Riverina for at least 40,000 years. In Narrandera, I saw considerable community acknowledgment of their contribution. The wall behind the information centre was decorated with Indigenous-themed murals. My friend Robyn, with her light-coloured hair and grey eyes, recently uncovered hidden Indigenous links to the original people of the Riverina. I can't help wondering about my own...

Rivers always played a significant role in the lifestyle of Wiradjuri peoples, providing food, a means of travel and trade. Murray cod and shellfish were gathered and bark canoes were crafted for travel. Their construction left scars still to be seen sometimes on river red gums and other trees along the banks.

As I enter Coolamon Shire, the sign reads, 'Big enough to serve. Small enough to care.' I like it. It lists the six main towns of the shire. I turn off left into the Ganmain Road. Now I am travelling in the same direction RFG was when he met a swagman with his dog.

Coolamon Shire

Ganmain, with a population of around 600, is some fifteen kilometres from Coolamon. I turn right into the town at the imposing two-storey verandaed hotel. I don't imagine either the tramp or my father ever went in there. One was an outcast, the other a teetotaller. In fact, neither of them touched alcohol – the one by profession; the other through having an alcoholic father who beat him.

This town was first named Boggy Creek, changing its name to Ganmain. How many boggy creeks, like station streets, must there be in Australia? Opposite the pub is the post office, a one-storey place resembling a family home with a porch and office room in front. In the mid to late nineteenth century, many country police stations too were constructed like this. The street-fronted rooms were accessible to the public.

In a way, as with the many other denominations, the Methodist minister's home served a similar function. It was usually next door to the church and attracted not only swagmen. Folk called to arrange weddings, funerals, home or hospital visits or simply to talk over life's dilemmas. The parsonage was often the venue for smaller church meetings too. People dropped in regularly, and weekends were often busiest of all. On Sunday, the main church service was usually in the late morning and the main meal was after church in the middle of the day – usually a roast dinner. Often, guests, family friends or visitors, were invited. In those days, almost everyone went to one church or the other.

I retrace my path back onto the main road east and arrive in Coolamon by late morning. It is not far. Coolamon is a very pleasant larger town with an exceptionally wide main street. This has a long strip of parkland down its centre. The weather has cleared and people are just out and about, it being Sunday. There are several upmarket eateries for them to choose from, including a hotel. I browse through a smart second-hand shop where I see mementos of my childhood, including a globite school case. How many hours, days, weeks, years, did I sit astride such a case waiting for a bus to school? While my father rode a horse to school, Sully received what little education he had on a ship.

I drive around and around endlessly. The township is spread out and bisected by another large thoroughfare. I can't spot a Methodist church anywhere. After a 'special' Coolamon pie, milkshake and a long walk up and down this delightful main street, I fill the car. Fuel is none too cheap at $1.32 a litre. (It's been $1.18 sometimes in Melbourne.)

Finally before I drive off, I locate what probably was the Methodist church. It is on the corner of two streets close to the main street and shops – very accessible for a mother and three young children. My brother, the youngest of the three, was born here. I imagine my mother, a young woman with another new baby. Beryl her eldest was born in 1926 at Boorowa. I haven't been there yet; it is further east and north of Coolamon.

My mother remembered the birth of their only son Ken while they lived at Coolamon, very well.

> We liked Coolamon very much, we always liked the country. We liked the church, we liked the people. We used to get dust storms there, inches deep sometimes, but we didn't mind, we liked the folk very well.

RFG and EMG with Beryl May, Boorowa, 1927

L–R: Ken, Raye and Beryl Gibson, all friends of Sully, late 1930s

There were two doctors when we went there but when Ken was thought to be on the way the old doctor was there. We never liked him; we'd heard some rather queer things about what he did with people who were sick. A woman who was having a child had lost the baby and herself through not being taken to hospital quickly enough. They had a little bit of a hospital there. There was a new doctor so we went to him. He arranged to come [for the birth] and then he suddenly shot off, sold his practice and left. I think the old doctor pushed him out... engineered all this.

We decided the only thing to do was to go to Wagga where there were plenty of very good doctors. And so we went to the doctor in Wagga and he told us of a lady who had a private hospital for babies so that's what happened. We organised that and when the time came I had to go and stay in Wagga a couple of weeks with a lady who took in boarders for that sort of thing. She was very nice and she had a nice daughter and so forth. I waited until it was time to go to hospital. The hospital was very nice indeed. It was just a little private hospital and lovely nurse. And the doctor was very good.

The birth was quite all right. I was in hospital. Cold country there and they had a great big roaring fire in my room when the baby was born. He discovered beforehand, which the other one hadn't, that Ken was coming feet first too.... I went in there the day before and he tried to turn the baby round but he couldn't. So he delivered the other way but there was no trouble or anything. He was very clever that doctor. Everyone knew him and talked about him, and the lady was very nice in the place too. She was a trained midwife and she had this hospital.... I think I only stayed a fortnight. You didn't stay long and I went back home.

In the meantime, Russ's mother had come to stay with us. She stayed with the two little ones, Raye and Beryl, and Russ. I know she got mixed in their singlets or something but that was all right – they were all right there. They stayed at home in Coolamon and then they came to see me while I was in hospital when the baby was born. And we had a lady who used to come and help in the house if we needed her. We had a young girl who loved to take the children out for walks. I don't know if we paid her or not, I doubt it. It would be very little if we did. She loved to take the kids for a walk – a little girl that belonged to the church, so we never had any trouble with help.

Anyway mother was there of course. She probably cooked because she liked to cook things that Russ liked... and then I went back home. I was all right. I never had that much trouble after babies come. After you've been a fortnight you sort of begin to do things and we had the help there if we needed it of course.

Well then, strange to say, I had a bad time after I had Ken for a while because I didn't have enough breast milk to feed him. Or thought I didn't. I think I did now… He cried and cried and I was worried and worried and worried and all I could do was ring the doctor back in Wagga. We didn't go to the other doctor. He wouldn't have come probably. But in the end he told me to put Ken on to formula, one of the baby things. Ken got all right but the first three or four months I don't know why he didn't die because I didn't know much about babies. Although I'd had two, but he came all right and we've got a picture of him on his first birthday and that's the first time that he looked anything like a decent looking baby.

Coolamon Methodist Church, 2015

Coolamon Methodist Church, side view, 2015

As I walk around the corner slowly, I notice the land surrounding the proud old red-brick Methodist church at Coolamon has been converted into an organic garden. Bales of hay are being unloaded from a truck as I pull in. My father would have liked that. Flowers, herbs and edible vegetables, intertwined, are thriving around the church. I recognise a house next door as the original parsonage, though no doubt it has changed hands since then and is now a private residence.

Out the back of the church is another building; perhaps it once was a church hall. It is being converted maybe as a workshop for handicapped people. There is a man with a walker watching the truck unload. By the time I return from photographing and exploring the front street, he has gone and so has the truck. I do not like to intrude, especially as I am not completely sure it was the Methodist church. I guess it is, though, and now that I have located old photos, I am sure of it.

Former Coolamon Methodist church and parsonage, 1930s

When RFG gave the tramp a lift into Ganmain (one of his many preaching places), he must have been comfortable in his new life as a clergyman, husband and father. Somehow he would have made time to plant vegetables. It was something he always did, a habit of his early life on the land – self-sufficiency. In Murwillumbah, the family raised not only dairy cattle but grew bananas and, for their personal use, paw paw, which in those days required both a male and female plant. RFG did enjoy a good paw paw (which these days many call papaya). He was not so fussy either about the condition of the bananas he ate – into old age. His grandchildren remember him as an old man eating brown and black bananas that no one else would consider edible.

On the farm: Vic (left) and Russ Gibson, Murwillumbah, 1916

Bananas had played an important part in RFG's early life. The income from them and the sale of the dairy farm the family owned provided for his religious training at Leigh College, after the death of his father.

> We had to see the solicitor and they had to apportion the property. Mother just said no, she wasn't having any, so it was divided between the two sons. It was up to us then to share it with our mother. It was sold within a couple of years. I had the roughest part I might have had more like 140 acres and Vic had the 100.
>
> Just before my father died we had a huge sale, sold up everything. He periodically did that. He'd stock up and then he'd sell up and hope to make 100 pounds or so to take off the debt. Then he'd commence buying up again. Well he'd sold up and I think he'd bought eight cows when he died. We had about eight cows and a huge property. We had a lot of young stock growing up. We made a bit of capital out of those. We bred everything that was worthwhile, killed all the young bulls and reared all the young heifers, they were more profitable. They came into milk when they were about three years old. So they were handy and they had calves too.
>
> We used to run most of our young stock on the property that I got over extra. It was all mountainous, really the side of a small mountain range and we'd cleared it enough to run all the young stock there. And bring them down when they had their first calf. They had to be brought down and broken into the milking yard. There were generally about 40 young heifers up there to replenish our herd as necessary. But I think we only had about the eight cows and they weren't all milking either when he died.

The last twelve months I was home. I did nothing but study for the ministry. We'd saved up pretty well Vic and I from selling bananas. I had somewhere I think it was a bit over one hundred pounds saved up from selling those. So they helped me a bit. But they didn't charge us really in college. It was all free. After I came to Sydney I had three years of study. Many of the men at that time only got two.

I got on very well with the Principal of Leigh College, Bennet. As a matter of fact he tried to get me as an assistant tutor. To train me enough but the Conference wouldn't let him. They wouldn't let me go. That's what I would have liked very much. It would have just suited me down to the ground.

From that time onwards until his retirement in 1966, my father's life was committed to the church. Despite his changing views on many issues, he did not shirk his responsibilities.

Perhaps, like me, RFG sometimes felt a twang of longing for the flexibility and freedom of a swagman's life. The respite it offered from the niceties of social obligations. (I haven't counted the number of times my mother's memoirs use that word – 'nice'.) Sully was released from many social constraints, a plethora of expectations. Whatever our time or place in humanity's unfolding saga, these expectations (sometimes strange or unnecessary ones) exist.

4

Wanderers

The countryside is easy and pleasant. I'm eager to press on, but which way? The day is fine now and the flat roads make driving easy. Birds, happy in random flight, celebrate the cessation of rain as they drift on the wind or dive down into green paddocks. It's the serendipity of the journey, whether the swagman's meanderings through country NSW, or my own odd attempts to piece together stories from the past.

Having slept reasonably well in the car the previous night, I feel a special kinship with Sully now and the ongoing freedom of his life. What does it matter if he camps near Coolamon, Ganmain or even sad little Grong Grong?

The lifestyle of Indigenous owners had largely been displaced before Sully's arrival in the country. The days of grey nomads, campervans, overseas tourists and backpackers were ahead. Neither that past nor this future had any bearing on the freedom and simplicity of Sully's life. Did he perhaps know something we have forgotten?

I had planned to follow a chronological pilgrimage but this, I can see now, isn't realistic. Every so often, my parents' life would diverge back to Sydney or somewhere else. They did not follow any geographically logical pattern in their employment moves. Does it matter if the sequence of NSW country towns I visit is random? In one way not at all, but in another way it matters to get it straight. I know that RFG himself would have endeavoured to sort out any project he was undertaking to the very best of his abilities – no half measures with him. And this is what Sully did too. To the best of his abilities and opportunities, he gave life his best shot.

Originally, I had planned to head due east from Coolamon to join the Olympic Highway at Junee and on to Wagga (officially Wagga Wagga). But the afternoon is full of promise now the skies have cleared. All the side roads I have taken so far have been flat and pleasant. Besides, I enjoy them more. Often mine is the only car on the road, which has left me free to saunter along, stop for an occasional smartphone photo or a pleasant roadside pee. So, when I notice a signpost to Temora, as I walk across the width of the gigantic Coolamon main street on the long way back to my car, I think, 'Why not'? There had been another circuit in between. As my mother recalls,

> We'd transhipped from Coolamon up to Mudgee and then we came back next door to Temora.

My parents had ranged far afield before returning to Temora, where I was now headed, just sixty kilometres from Coolamon.

Once a year, all the Methodist ministers in NSW would gather for their Annual Conference in Sydney, at the Lyceum Theatre. There the destiny of all those ministers to be moved was decided. Perhaps their three years in one place was up or, for various other reasons, they needed to move. Neither my father nor mother much approved of the randomness of such decisions. Or perhaps what they really disapproved of was that they were not as random as they should have been. RFG recalls,

> They sent you where they liked. But if a senior man put up a good tale and most of them could put up a good tale that they couldn't get on too well, they'd push you out of it as a young man… It was published in a Methodist newspaper. You had to say you were invited. And if you were invited you were put down and in the first reading for that place. But there were three readings and these chaps that wanted something and were older they always got someone from their side to nominate them. And then you had to stand for the vote and it was voted on at the conference. You had to stand the vote of about 150 ministers… But they didn't mind telling half-truths either if they wanted to put up a case against you. Or put up a case for their seniority to get their point. Half truth would be better than a full one always… minister or no minister. … All legal.

RFG was, among clergymen at least, considered something of a financial wizard. Frequently he would be appointed to a circuit with financial worries. Somewhere a former minister and the council of 'circuit stewards' who ran the district and its churches had overspent on new facilities, renovations or church appeals. Or, as happened more by the time I arrived on the scene, there were too few regular members to keep finances afloat easily.

All his adult life, RFG was troubled by kidney disease. In 1924, before his marriage, he had been so ill that his fiancée came down to visit him in Berrigan.

Muriel Shield beside RFG's new Ford, Berrigan circuit, 1924

After their marriage and three years at Boorowa, they were transferred back to Sydney so RFG would be close to medical treatment when needed. Reluctantly he became the second minister in the Leichhardt circuit, at the Austenham Road church. It was there the second daughter, Phyllis Rae (now Raye), was born.

Leichardt was also the place his wife, Enid Muriel Gibson (EMG), had lived for many of her teenage years. Muriel's mother, Jessie Shield (née Hollands), had died of cancer in Leichhardt in 1918. She was only forty-seven.

Reginald Shield, Muriel's elder brother, had enlisted in March 1916, almost the exact time my father had failed to do so. Reg served all through the war in France in the 3rd Divisional Cyclist Company, AIF. I had no

Jessie Amy Hollands (later Shield), c. 1895

Jessie Amy Shield just before her death from cancer, 1918

This isn't half a 'windy' place !
Il y a plutôt de l'orage par ici !

Avec les compliments d'une de vos jolies alliées.
Greetings from one of your fair Allies.

Postcards from France, World War I, front (above) and back (opposite)

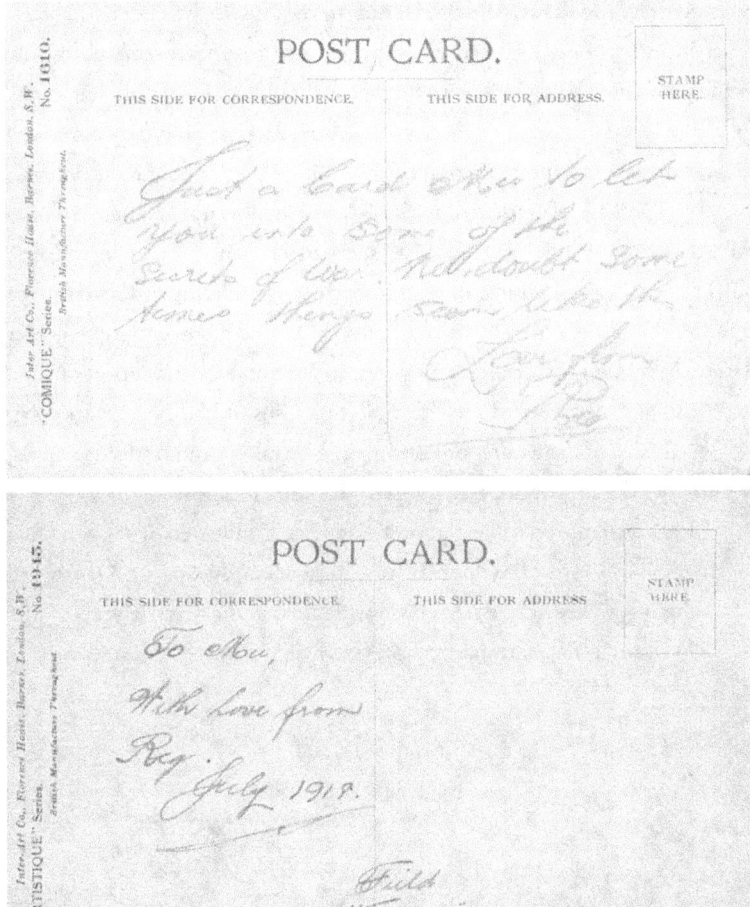

idea there was a cyclist division till I began this pilgrimage. Reg sent irregular postcards to his mother and sister and I still have them today.

Reg's mother had died some months before her only son returned from World War I. He was informed of her death on the return ship. Only Muriel was left to meet her brother Reg when he disembarked at Sydney on 13 July 1919 (his father had gone to work in Samoa). It was pouring with rain. Muriel remembers she was drenched. Reg had been gassed several times. His army medical records list scabies and syphilis during his years on the French front. They provide no other information.

He was one of so many. Though he did survive, his life was not a long one.

Muriel was only eighteen when her mother died. She remembers that same year, 1918, being so ill with flu that she could not see the adored Prince of Wales when he visited University of Sydney. I wonder if it may have been the deadly Spanish influenza that the returning troops brought with them.

In 1920, Muriel graduated with a BA and then completed her Diploma of Education. While at university, she had chosen to train in the first Girl Guide Leaders course offered in Sydney, graduating at Government House. She went on to form the first Girl Guide troop in Cooma. Her later work with girls' church clubs was, in a sense, a continuation of this.

Leichardt was also where she and Russ Gibson had been married in 1925. This was not the first or last time the couple would find themselves, sometimes decades apart, returning to the same locations.

RFG's first probationary appointment as a minister of religion had been at Bulli, south of Sydney. It was extraordinarily close to Dapto and Wollongong, where he had been born and raised in the first five years of life.

RFG's maternal grandfather Griffin owned Kemble Grange, a large

James French and Leah Griffin, c. 1880

Victor (standing) and Russell Gibson, Dapto, c. 1900

The two grave memorials side by side, old Brownsville Anglican churchyard

dairy property in the area. His grandfather Gibson had several properties, all dairy farms, around the same area by the time he died. Both were Anglicans. Some years before, I had been surprised to find two imposing monumental graves with inscriptions for James Griffin and Edward Gibson – RFG's two grandfathers (with their respective wives appended). They loomed large in the front line of graves, almost side by side in the early Brownsville Anglican church cemetery. It was as if in death each was competing with the other to erect a prosperous, lasting memorial.

RFG's father John Gibson had been a staunch Orangeman, though RFG himself had no interest at all. I assume that his father, a lowland Scot, immigrating to Australia from Northern Ireland in the 1850s, was an Orangeman too. After the battle of the Boyne, many lowland Scots, troublesome to the English and their new German Protestant king, were encouraged to migrate to Northern Ireland. There they occupied lands left by all the slaughtered local Roman Catholics who had supported the cause of the descendants of James II the deposed Stuart monarch. When the potato blight affected crops in Ireland, many migrated to Australia, (and elsewhere). Probably the Gibsons were part of this exodus.

5

War and peace

Again I am on a bitumen road with no central line marker – a country road travelled by Sully and my father (though no longer of compacted earth) with the same low-branching eucalypts and sheoaks. I pass paddock after paddock of lush green canola plants – a new seed crop since those early days. It's good pasture land; a few sheep remain here and there. It must have been a lovely region to walk and rest in, carrying a swag or boiling up the billy.

Coolabahs and other trees are plentiful enough for slinging a swag and making a pleasant camp. Not the tall trees I am used to from Tasmania but stumpy eucalypts whose thinner trunks bifurcate lower down. Laneways, named for the owners of each property, run off at right angles to the bitumen. Here too, each one has a roadside letter box perched on a post.

I dawdle along the Temora road. It becomes dull again as I amble through what at various times must have been cattle and sheep country and possibly still is in parts. The land is, of course, fenced – so vital to any property. In his youth, my father and his elder brother Vic had sometimes gone out all day fencing:

> We put up fences too. Some of the time we'd leave in the morning we'd go off fencing and take our dinner with us. Put up about 14 posts in the day between milking time and have to come home at about 3 o'clock to bring the cows in and get milking again. We were always pretty busy. Every wet day we went shooting birds and wallabies. We got a bit of extra pocket money for the wallaby skins, that's why we shot them.

Sully too, over the course of his nomadic rover's life, had dug in fence posts and strained the wires taut between them. Sometimes he'd work for days, even weeks. The young RFG was swift and efficient, part of a two-lad team. The swagman often worked alone at a different pace. Yet both men shared knowledge of the common day to day work necessary to maintain a country property.

As I drive, I notice Cootamundra wattle in bloom. Its lovely clusters of golden balls are welcome beside the road. Joyous colour in the dull afternoon.

Before long, I angle park in the imposing main street of Temora, not as wide as Coolamon's main street but Temora is a larger town with an urban population of around 4,000. I imagine 'Temora' is a local indigenous name but no, apparently it's Celtic and means something like 'an eminence commanding a wide view'.

As it's winter, I know the evening will close in soon. I will go no further today, even though it's still mid-afternoon. Where I park, I notice an interesting sign offering accommodation at reasonable rates behind the main street. Probably it's at the back of the old two-storey buildings in front of me. The sign implies the proprietor can be reached by phone if not in the office at the rear. I have no idea how to get through to the rear of the old shopfronts. There's no obvious passage between them.

As so often when in doubt, I drive to the nearby supermarket. Coles or Woolies, it's always hit or miss which one of the two grocery giants has cornered the bulk of shoppers in each new place. There are a lot of cars coming and going but I find a parking spot in a distant corner.

The night before in the rain and dark, I'd wondered why my low-beam right-side headlight had been so dim. I'd been forever dipping and raising the beam for a stream of oncoming road trains carrying goods between Victoria, NSW and the Hay Plains into SA. Checking in the car park, I find that the globe has ceased to function on low beam – no wonder I couldn't see. That will need to be fixed before I attempt any night driving. Along the journey, I've noticed so many vehicles approaching me with only one headlight. So it isn't just a Tasmanian phenomenon.

I look up other accommodation places, and then give Theresa a final call. She answers. Had I rung before? The whole family – herself, husband and children – are having a monster house clean-out on their property just out of town. She will be in to meet me in forty minutes. There are several rooms available at $50 a night with breakfast included. She will bring a cooked breakfast in with her next morning while dropping her youngest at the local Roman Catholic school nearby. There are half a dozen railway workers staying in the other wing of the old building, she explains. They won't bother me, she assures, as they leave for work at 6 a.m. each day. No en suites – it is an old place – but I will have sole use of the bathroom and toilet on what will be my side. I am intrigued, curious even. She sounds friendly and helpful. I am sure she is an honest person. She sounds very straightforward and open.

This is the first of many happy encounters with south-western NSW. I've entered a different world. I am used to the pace, manner and lifestyle of the eastern seaboard from Wollongong to Brisbane. Even the smaller seaside towns are holiday destinations and represent a brash new Australia. Here, inland, the other side of the Great Dividing Range, I am beginning to recognise something authentic and fundamentally decent. A consideration for others. Dependable people I might befriend within five minutes and trust for life.

Temora has been reported as being the friendliest town in New South Wales and I would agree, though many other towns I visit are also welcoming and helpful. My mother had always known this country kindness:

> I don't think we were really cut out for city churches in a sense – we both fitted in better with old fashioned country places and people.

My father's reflections expressed it a little differently:

> I liked Coolamon, I liked Temora. Coolamon was a huge circuit 16 preaching places. It was a happy place because I liked all those circuits and all those people they were very nice people. They'd do anything for me at all.
>
> But I must say I was happy in practically all my circuits. It's hard to say which I liked best. The hardest circuit I ever had was Coolamon and I liked it perhaps the best of all. I enjoyed myself there. I believe I stayed five years

there; still it was very hard work but I liked it quite well. I was generally invited to stay an extra year everywhere I went.

Now I too see that folk who were not in an unnecessary hurry (often a mark of self-importance anyway), are far more agreeable to be around. They don't charge outrageously for every little unreasonable thing either. In big cities, I am now charged for the tiny plastic bottles of soy sauce with my sushi roll. There is always something extra to add a tab charge onto if that is your goal.

Freshly showered and comfortable, snuggled up with the heater on in my room, I read a little about Temora. It began as a pastoral station in 1847 then in 1869 gold was found. Ten years later, 20,000 people thronged the gold diggings at Temora, where the famous Mother Shipton nugget was found, weighing 308 ounces. The Temora railway station opened in 1893. At the time of the first Australian census in 1911, with the collapse of the goldfield, the population had dropped to 2,784. Then in the early twentieth century, the Temora area was settled by people of German descent. Today, together with a variety of agricultural and farming industries including wheat, canola and sheep, it is the second largest honey producer in Australia.

The following morning, I consume every bit of a large plate of bacon, mushroom, baked beans, tomato (all fresh produce) plus toast and Earl Grey tea. That should keep me fuelled. As Theresa washes up and serves me another cup and more toast, we share an interesting and, for me, informative conversation.

When I explain the purpose of my journey, she recalls how her own mother's family welcomed strangers in the Depression. Her mother too often spoken of these times. The family had a room for travellers outside but attached to their farmhouse. The room did not allow entry into the main part of the house. Travellers were welcomed, especially in those needy depression times, with a cup of tea and a good feed. Country hospitality was provided at many places as the dispossessed moved on or stayed a little while to help with needed odd jobs.

In a very real sense, Theresa was her mother's daughter. The night before while I enjoyed the warmth of the fire (if not so much the TV) in the dining room, I encountered a local, recently parted from wife and family. He was staying till his house was sold. A gourmet cook evidently, he was skinning red peppers and preparing fresh field mushrooms for a wonderfully creative meal that involved stuffing macadamia nuts under the outer skin of a chicken to be baked.

The railway crew, mostly work-for-the-dole lads from the Central Coast were anxious to meet the requirements of their salaried employment. They'd settled down early the night before. A friendly, respectful group of men (as Theresa had assured me), they were tired from a full day out in the country replacing railway sleepers. In the morning, they had backed their truck out of the yard before I was entirely awake. They drove out into the back lane, parallel to the main street. The night before, I'd found my way in there, past the back of the police premises. This made me feel safe too. When the men had returned from work around 5 p.m., they'd blocked me in. I'd assured them I wouldn't be leaving before 6 a.m. Possibly I'd used their chosen spot inadvertently but they were unperturbed and made no grumbles.

Theresa's son is ten years or so younger than her other children. 'Change of life baby,' I remarked, using the phrase I'd heard my mother use so often to describe me. She tells me that often near menopause, women give birth after a long break in childbearing. It's because the ovaries give a final burst and express more than one egg at a time. I had never heard this scientific explanation before. It was a revelation. The female body, preparing for menopause, ejects not one but several eggs at a time. So that's why.

When ineptitude prevents me from using Mr Google's phone maps, Theresa kindly allows my car to follow hers to a reliable local mechanic on the outskirts of Temora. His name indicates German heritage. Much to my relief, for around $20 my faulty headlight is replaced. Vastly relieved that it was nothing more complicated, I head off for Harden. I am already on the road heading east out of town. Harden is where Mr Sully lost his swagman's corked hat in the eddies of the Murrumbidgee River.

As far as I know, Sully had very little direct connection with either of the great wars. My parents did, though, and it was in Temora that they both experienced the lows and highs of World WarII. My mother remembers,

> Temora was a busy time because the Second World War had started. It started while we were in Mudgee but we never had much to do with it then. But by the time we got up to Temora they'd just constructed a huge aerodrome for training pilots.

Temora was the location of many wartime memories both my parents shared later. But my mother's first memory of arriving in town was not of war but of the Temora agricultural show.

> In country towns you have a huge Show once a year for the townspeople. And when we got to Temora somebody in the Church Aid said it was coming close to the time. The churches had taken it in turns before our time to do all the show catering and it was our turn the week or so after we arrived.
>
> Maybe it wasn't that close but soon after we got to Temora when I went to the Ladies Church Aid meeting they said, oh we'll soon be really busy because we've got the show coming on.
>
> 'The show,' I said, 'how can we do that'? I wondered how we could manage a whole great Show … Anyway when we came to getting church aid ready they had all this stuff spread out. There were men, women and children there. We had about 49 plum puddings provided by all the country folk round the district. We had sandwiches to sell to everybody that came to the Show. We had everything you can imagine, if you've ever been to a country show, you'll know what a huge thing it was. What it involved. And our church aid ladies did the whole of it.
>
> The Presbyterians and the Anglicans had done it, they got tired of it I think. But we had it and then of course we got the war on top of us. .. I didn't do much cooking I think I was given something easy to prepare but they had about 40 puddings there and when it came the day of the Show you went the night before and got all the tables ready and all of that three days the Show was on there'd be about 100 men boiling water troughs outside and cooking puddings and you've no idea what it was like. But it went like that. They'd done it so much and so often. It was marvellous really. It was an eye opener to me.

The No. 10 Elementary Flying Training School (10 EFTS) was set up by the Royal Australian Air Force (RAAF) in May 1941. No. 10 EFTS was the largest and longest lived of the flying schools established under the Empire Air Training Scheme during World War Two (WWII). Throughout WWII more than 10,000 personnel were involved at the school with upwards of 2,400 pilots being trained. At its peak the unit contained a total of 97 de Havilland Tiger Moth aircraft. Four satellite airfields were set up around the Temora district to cope with the demand to train RAAF pilots. No 10 EFTS ceased operation on 12 March 1946 making it the last WWII flying school to close. My parents by some curious chance found themselves there over almost this entire period.

EMG remembers,

> After they started the Air Force base and we got the war going badly, the next Show we gave all the money to them. When the war was well on we had this elementary training college for pilots and there were groups of men coming to be trained as pilots and off they'd go to the war to get killed or whatever. But also all the ground staff and all the trainers were there. It was a terrific thing.

Sully was living in a shed very close to the family in Temora, as he had been in Mudgee. It was in Temora that he was so upset to witness little Kenny fall from the loft. He sometimes attended church too in his new suit purchased with his pension money. Perhaps he was at those wartime funerals. My father later recalled,

> I was at Temora during most of the war. In fact I was a chaplain in the Air Force. For two years I was chaplain at the air school. I had the circuit – so it was just overtime. I was at the war as a chaplain.
>
> Even for the three years I was chaplain; I had to run a circuit and couldn't let up there. Being a chaplain was just an extra. I'd go out, I think it was one day a week I used to go out and put in at the camp. But most of them I liked very much. In fact I got in as a chaplain because they had a very awkward chap as a Church of England man that was there. He was always trying to put something over them. If the drinks were going round he'd probably keep pretty quiet and get them all free. The officers were pretty shrewd. I think he drank a bit too much too.

The officers, the chaplains were with the officers' mess always, and he was known as being a good drinker. But they don't respect a good drinker. They pretend they do, but even the officers mistrust a chap that drinks much. That may be natural but I was rather surprised, I didn't know they would. They came and asked me if I'd become chaplain on that score. They didn't make it public that they disliked this chap but they did. And as far as I was concerned I got on well with them. They could take too much if they wanted to, not many of them did, but they could if they wanted to. It was all right for them but not all right for the Padre. They were a good crowd.

The men completed their flying instruction there and the officers often went away. There was one chap I don't know if he ever came back. He wanted to get to Darwin. He got up to Darwin all right. But I never heard… There were lots of casualties there, I don't know if he came back.

Most of them were very nice chaps; I was quite fond of them. They'd always chip me when I went into the bar for sure, because I'd have a ginger ale or lemonade or something like that. It was always soft. And I'd generally get a cry from someone. Hey padre, that'll rot your boots. I got that often. But you just took that. They didn't mean any harm they were just throwing off at the Padre because he took soft stuff.

As the minister's wife, my mother was busy at Temora. She remembers many sad and happy times during her war years there.

We used to have twenty or thirty come to church. We used to have five or six to dinner nearly every Sunday. Not that that worried me. I mean you just cooked what you had and Dad was with us a bit then. We always cooked a roast dinner and roast potatoes and Dad would keep an eye on the oven. You never knew if you'd bring three home, or if there were ten people, air [force] people, at church. I'd take two or three, or somebody would take two or three out in the country or someone else would take three or four somewhere else. We always gave them their dinners. But we never knew who we were going to have.

It was a lovely time in a way. It wasn't a lovely time because war was on and a lot of those boys got killed… not all. But it was. And Russ became … well he was acting chaplain all the while he was there and he loved it as a matter of fact.

And at the same time he'd been going to Masonic lodges all his life but he'd never been long enough in the one place to get to the top of the tree. Worthy Brother, Worshipful Master or something… While he was there he actually was head of that too because a lot of the younger men had gone to the war and some of the others were not there, so he took that on too. He had a very busy time there and some sad times.

One day there we had three chaps killed in the war. One of our own people, one was a Catholic and one some other church. We had the mother of this young chap that had been killed. She was a lovely person... They were all buried in their own church but they met together and all went out to the cemetery there. It was a sad time but it was a very interesting good time in a sense...

Later on a minister's wife died too while we were there. You meet everything in these places but we loved Temora it was a good place and it's no distance from Wagga as well as from Coolamon the other place where we had been.

And the pilots of course were only there for about six weeks or whatever it was they'd take the training, and then they'd go off and another lot come. We met a lot of nice men. There was one man we used to write to who played the organ in our church, Tom Brown. He was training but it wasn't to fly, there were a lot of other things. He was there for years and some of the others too, we'd always have a lot coming to church.

Then after church they'd have singing or something, singing hymns, you'd have a crowd there too. Country people were always willing to take two or three home and give them their dinner if they wanted to. In a way it was a happy time a really interesting time. There were one or two other men we got very much involved with, whom I knew very well. We got to know the pilots to but some of them went off and some got killed and some didn't. There was one Beryl [EMG's eldest daughter was a teenager by then] knew, that she thought she was fond of once. He got killed.

Today, Temora has an aviation museum dedicated to aircraft and pilots who had defended Australia. It continues its aviation heritage as a preferred airfield for activities including gliding, parachuting, aerobatics, ultra-light aircraft operations and model aircraft.

While running the church and being a padre in the air force, RFG found time for other things around Temora too. Perhaps in this he was just a little influenced by Mr Sully.

What I enjoyed there I'd have a big party of boys, ten to fifteen mostly. I used to take them out camping every now and then. I'd be onto a farmer to

A camping trip: RFG with OKs, Temora, c. 1940

let us go onto his property. We'd take that tent and we'd pitch it and they'd make their own beds and it taught them a bit too. I knew pretty well about camping and the boys did before I'd finished too.

We'd pick a place about eight or nine miles out of town and go out mostly for three days or even four days to camp and cook our own meals. I made them all take their own food. Each one had to take food and look after it. It seemed the only way to do it with fifteen boys camping.

I had one boy in particular that was a bit greedy. He was quite a nice chap, but he used to pick on a little chap. One little chap, his mother had a shop and he used to bring all sorts of particularly nice things – especially nice things- and they discovered that they were disappearing. Well this chap, he usen't to steal them. No he wasn't that sort. But he used to demand them off the boy. And the boy was about nine and he was about fifteen. The boy always gave them to him. It came to my notice. I had to deal with that and stop it. Strangely enough the big chap is still a friend of mine. If ever he gets a chance to enquire of where I am and what's happening to me. His brother's a member of parliament. I better not say the name…. but he's in parliament in Canberra [1983]. He was a very nice chap the brother I liked him very much.

There are more memories from their time in Temora than most other places for both RFG and EMG. My mother remembers another incident that she had to deal with herself because my father was absent.

Another sad thing was we had very nice friends in the country, some we still write to. There was a family we knew very well a mother and father. I think the father had died and the mother was there. There was a grown up family but there was one girl, in her 30s. She'd never got married, the others had.

While the war was on one of the staff, one of the air force chaps we got to know well and who came to the church all the time began to like her. He was about the same age. He wasn't learning to fly. He was in some of the other part of it. In the end they married and we thought, now isn't that lovely, because she was getting on a bit. She hadn't met anyone else. I suppose in the country you don't see all that many young people....

It was a sad thing because she got married and he took her back down to Melbourne. He'd come from Melbourne. A nice chap and so was she, they went away to Melbourne. After, I don't know, could have been six months, she came back and so did he. She came back and she was getting sick. I think she might have been too old to get married. I don't know what it was. Anyway she came back to her mother and sister who had married and lost her husband before.

They got the doctor, the doctor who we knew was quite strange. Though we liked him all right, there were better ones. He eventually put her into the hospital. There was a private hospital in Temora next door to where they all learnt to swim. That's how our lot all leant to swim. It was a beautiful swimming pool in Temora. They'd never been near any water in their life before. They all learnt to swim there...

These things happen that way. Russ was down at conference in Sydney which he had to go to because he was Chairman of the District there, and this lass, the married girl who had lost her husband before said we don't know what's become of my sister (who had married this nice chap from Melbourne).

Something went wrong with her...so everyone went looking and do you know where they found her? She'd climbed up on the big wire fence around the baths and jumped in. And eventually that's what had happened. Drowned herself. She was sure she had cancer. The doctor was sure she didn't. I don't know. We knew that doctor pretty well and he had different ideas and I don't think he might perhaps have treated her as easily as some...

I know it was dreadful and the girl's sister came up to me. And my dad was with me then. He'd stopped going to work much and he was up there for a while and she came up to me and said, 'they've found my sister...' She had climbed up the top and jumped in apparently. Of course if you wanted to do it I suppose you could and she was a country girl anyway.

So I went back down with her [the sister] to the old mother and herself and the son they had. I stayed the night. My dad kept an eye on our family. They were all right anyway, Russ was over at conference...so then I went down and this same doctor who had funny little ways. He came in and he said, now look… They'd come in from the country but they lived in Temora and he said, 'who are your greatest friend out there…you ring them up and tell them to come in to you now'. There'd be a funeral of course in a little while. It was a stupid thing to say in some ways. Anyway, the family came in. I'd stayed there that night…it upset us all a bit and it explained the sort of thing the doctor did do. It was silly, they were friends but all friends come around you when you need it [without being ordered to].

RAAF wartime funeral, Temora; RFG at far right of casket

One or two other things he did were strange… [I expect it was he too who ordered my mother to have all my sister's front teeth pulled on her sixteenth birthday, when she had bad stomach pains.]

I had to get on to where Russ was staying in Sydney. It took me a long time to get hold of Russ to see if he could come back for the funeral. Of course they were real church people. But he couldn't because he was chairman and he had to do certain things for the ministers in his own district… so he told me to ring a very nice man who hadn't gone to conference.

I had to go and ring this man and explain what had happened that this girl who we loved very much had married this young chap and they were a good couple, but she'd killed herself and would he come and take the funeral. So he came and took the funeral. He couldn't have given a better funeral if he'd known for a year before what he had to preach on. It's not easy to take a funeral like that…

The husband came up. They were a nice family. It's just that somehow the marriage didn't fit. Probably from the girl being late in life to start to marry… or whether she didn't fit in with the parents… they were all quite happy about it everybody was and so were we. We thought it was a nice thing that ever happened to her because she was getting on…but that's just how it happened…

It was one of the nicest sermons and the whole town was there. There were all the Methodists of course. This man came and took the service and buried her… I'd stayed all night with her people that night because they were on their own…

That's the sort of thing; it was a very exciting place in a sense. I don't mean exciting in a nice way, it wasn't. But there were lots of things happened.

6

Another trail

Sully had moved to Temora from Mudgee alongside RFG's family. After Harden, I'm heading for Mudgee, via Boorowa. It looks quite a distance on the map. I want to stop at Harden, not because there's much of immediate interest for a casual passerby, but because it's the place where Sully lost his corked swagman's hat.

It's a pleasant morning's journey from Temora. As I drive blue sky brakes through then clouds over again. I pass sloping plains, green pasture with cattle and pigs one side, sheep on the other. This part of the Riverina is clearly very fertile. Small hills in the distance make an appealing view. Harden itself is situated in a dip between small hills hugging the Murrumbidgee River.

As I draw closer to Harden, the country changes from very flat to gently undulating. I pull into a parking area – something between a park and a truck rest stop. The water remains dull and uninteresting. Rain starts then eases. The river is grey and uninviting now. I try to picture poor Sully's hat floating down the Murrumbidgee, just out of reach, to snag near the far bank where he will never reach it. A comic tragedy.

Though I've missed the town of Cootamundra by sidetracking to Harden, all around me still are the wattles that bear its name. Glowing glorious yellow, these wattles were adopted, with their rich green foliage, as Australia's national flower and her national colours. I recall John Howard and his wattle sprig buttonholes (now every prime minister wears them). Though not of the same political persuasion, John Howard must have been in my father's Methodist scripture classes as a lad at Canterbury Boys

High, Sydney. This time, RFG had received an invitation to Hornsby. That was the way of things… He was instead sent to Hurlstone Park/Canterbury.

Now, out of sequence, I am heading further east to Boorowa, where the family had lived before Coolamon. The gently folding paddocks and scattered trees look drier here at this time of year. Boorowa was the first posting of my newlywed parents. My eldest sister Beryl was born here.

No doubt the swagman passed through Boorowa too but it is not one of the places that my father recalled meeting him. It was not war stories that I grew up on but this list of country parsonages, places my parents and older siblings had lived with assorted dogs, friends and quite often with Mr Sully nearby (see appendix).

By the time I arrive at Boorowa, I am all churched out. I make a desultory drive around the spread-out town. Eventually, down on the flat a little away from the main streets, I locate a smallish brick Methodist church. Again it stands on a corner block with the side street containing what I take to have been the original parsonage. But there is a dog inside the yard barking ferociously, straining against the fence gate as I draw near. Clearly the house has been sold off and is now in private hands. The church too appears to be receiving minimal care.

I drive north, making an extensive burst of long-distance driving, towards Cowra. Wanting to press on again, I skirt the city itself and push on to Bathurst. School is coming out, traffic queues across intersections. It's almost as congested as a capital. I drive around and around, trying to locate another back road – this time to Mudgee. I've been successful all the way through the Riverina, taking the roads less travelled. I want to continue.

When my father came from Coolamon to Mudgee, it was not the place he expected to be sent.

> I was specially asked to go to Albury and I wanted to go there but the chap I worked with in Leichardt, thought he should get a very good circuit. And he wasn't getting one so he thought he had better call on Albury than I had. He got some of his older friends, he was a much older man, to push me

out of Albury and he got it. I knew folk, there, I'd been asked down there to preach once or twice. A chap that I knew very well was living there as a school teacher and he wanted me to go. That's why I had a good pull and I would have left and gone there but this old beggar put seniority ahead and pushed me out.

Once RFG got to Mudgee, however, it was a different matter.

I liked Mudgee it was a very nice place really. An old town. It had a lot of history but they were very nice folk. I was very happy there.

My mother gave another reason for RFG's appointment to Mudgee.

We stayed on in Coolamon until we were sent down to Mudgee. Russ had been invited to go to Albury but they sent him to Mudgee instead… somebody wanted somebody else to go there or something. They did a bit of that. They do it now worse than they ever did. But we always went wherever we were sent, we never worried.

I know we were nearly late getting there because it's a long way to Mudgee. But anyway we got to Mudgee and we liked Mudgee very well. It was a beautiful church but I know why Russ went there. He was one of the few ministers that understood finance. Mudgee bank, the ordinary bank, was going to foreclose because the church had such a bad debt and they couldn't pay it off.

The man before us who'd been a very good minister…knew nothing much about finance. They're not supposed to know about finance… But the man before the last minister had insisted on a piece of land in the main street. They had three or four shops built on it; but the trouble is they couldn't let them. Not properly and they were in a bad way.

Eventually I think they sold a couple. But that was why Russ, instead of going to Albury as he's been invited to, was sent to Mudgee – because he understood finance. He did know. When he got there the man at the bank said they'd foreclose if something was not done about it. Which they'd told the others too I suppose. But Russ of course he did a lot of work. And it worked out because in the end before we left Mudgee they'd paid off their debt and they'd collected enough money to put lovely stained-glass windows in the church…they had this big beautiful church because we helped to fix it up and it got better fixed up after we left. They were beautiful windows, I loved those windows…

Russ was very good with anything like that and he does understand that sort of thing. They all knew that too. Anyway we were five years at Mudgee. It was a busy place. A long way from Sydney or anywhere but we still liked it.

And now, though it's getting late in the afternoon, I decide to go there for the night. I find the petrol prices in Bathurst up by thirty cents on what I'd seen earlier. I'd become lost so many times and dense traffic had prevented me turning where I wanted. This country traveller was pining for another gentle country road. Little did I know what lay before me...

If I'd been even the slightest bit familiar with this part of inland NSW, I would have realised the difficulty I was having finding the back road to Mudgee was because it was not much used.

The heat of the middle of the day is dwindling as I set off with only a quarter tank of petrol. I calculate roughly on the map that this will be enough to cover the kilometres. In the shadow of the hills and trees, I wind down the window, turn off the aircon I'd needed in the hot city traffic and enjoy the gentle breeze. The radio is talking about some new tertiary institution – a female member of staff is expanding on its creative benefits.

Unheeding, I push on until gradually I realise the road is steadily climbing upwards and shows no signs of levelling out. I push the automatic overdrive button in to give more power for the climb. That will use more fuel too.

On and on, the road climbs, between steep mountains. Eventually I come to the strangest-looking township. It's constructed from red-brown wood and many houses are two-storeyed. It looks like snow country. There's a river with a bridge across a ravine on the far side of the town. I pull in and wait as a large truck tries to pass. There's a vehicle attempting to pull out in front of me from this peculiar township. Beside the road is a large sign declaring, 'No fuel available – do not ask'. Why hadn't I filled up at the tiny roadside shop some kilometres back where the price was twenty cents more than Bathurst? Well, that's why.

I drive in a loop around the curious settlement realising it was once an old gold mining place. An intoxicated group of ageing alternative

On the high road to Mudgee

lifestylers wave. Sure, you should get fuel – just seven kilometres off the main road. They smile, with mellow good will. 'But don't let them ignore you. Just toot and stand up for yourself.'

Surely it's worth it, to get petrol, I think. Or is it? I have used a lot of fuel and it's still a long way down from the top of the mountains to join the Mudgee road. Uncertainly, I diverge from the direct road through the mountains and head left – vaguely west. It's not the direction I want. Almost as soon as I divert, I begin to doubt my decision. It's bleak but grand on the narrow road – awesome country with towering cliffs and deep ravines. There's a suspension bridge across a far deeper ravine here and only one narrow lane. It's scary. If it was to break with my car on it, I would plunge far far below. I become full of fear. Irrational thoughts plague my mind and won't go away. I grip the wheel tightly, much too desperately, trying to keep in the centre and not knock the sides. Is it swaying?

Along the way, I read assorted unwelcoming signs such as 'Private property keep out' and 'No stopping here' or 'No roadside camping'. These are anything but reassuring. I pass a new upmarket accommodation sign and a long driveway but it looks deserted now. It's probably only a summer destination. 'Closed', the gate says. Is this where I should try to drive in for petrol? I don't know and it too says, 'Do not enter'. Cliffs tower above. I feel very small. The absent owners of vacant properties, huts and occasional houses harass me with their signs. This whole area is conspiring against me. I feel menaced by geography and human hostility. What should I do?

Perhaps I'd made a big mistake crossing that one-lane suspension bridge. It's more than seven kilometres from the 'main' road through the mountain. What should I do now? Eleven kilometres on, I decide to turn back. The road seems narrower. If I go on, it will be another thirty kilometres or more to reach somewhere I'd never heard of and can't locate on my map.

My hands are less and less steady on the wheel. I begin to shake uncontrollably. It's not something I'm used to, this panic. Conscious that evening is not far off, I debate with myself. If my car, elderly as it is, should stop here, who would come by? What could happen to this also elderly female stranded here alone? If nothing else, the night will be very very cold.

Like Sully on the mountain road between Armidale and Kempsey, I begin to feel very afraid. If he quickly shrugged off his concern and carried on, I could not. My mobile phone is, of course, well out of range among the mountains. Some cliff faces are sliced with mining. They hang far above this insignificant road. On the way back, I reread the unwelcoming signs and discover more of them. It all further undermines my confidence.

Eventually I return to the township I'd started from, the near-abandoned ghost mining town, resurrected by eccentrics. I decide there is no help here. Besides, I feel a fool. I'm becoming more and more introverted in my irrationality. Across the bridge, I pull over to allow a giant truck that comes roaring along to pass. Guess he's getting up speed for the incline ahead. The truck is carrying the largest cylindrical pipe I've ever seen. It's the size of a small house and as long as two. What will happen to me if it happens to come loose and roll off? I follow this truck like a duckling its mother. As I drive, I try to talk myself into a state of calm. By now, the fuel gauge is in the empty region. I'd travelled considerably over 400 kilometres and don't yet know the maximum capacity of this vehicle that's fairly new to me.

After ten or twenty kilometres of following the pipe truck, my reality brain has lapsed into oblivion. It could be 300 kilometres the way I feel. Finally we come to the intersection with the somewhat more main road. I turn north to Mudgee. Surely if I run out of fuel now, it won't matter so much. I'll be all right. I'm back in mobile range. I grab for my water bottle and drain it dry. There's no time to stop to get something to eat from the back, night is falling fast. I need to get safely into town.

That truck was my saviour, though he may never have known it. With his heavy load, he couldn't get far ahead of me and the knowledge that he was a fellow traveller there within sight leading me onward helped me regain some calm after the terror I'd experienced in those deserted mountains.

I limp thankfully into Mudgee just on empty as night falls. Parking somewhere near the main street, I lay back in my seat. For the moment, I am too exhausted to make any plan or find food. My large breakfast and a few nibbles have kept me going all day, sort of. I don't care what happens next. I am in Mudgee and alive. My car has made it.

How could I have been so foolish? Alone – no one in the world knew just where I was until I sent a panicked sms to my daughter when I got back within range. I had completely misjudged the country. Here was no Riverina gentle flatness. Unaware, I had wandered into some of the steepest, most isolated and magnificent mountains of eastern Australia – the Great Diving Range. Gold country, no less.

Now here I am in Mudgee. When I'm able to take notice, I see it is large and thriving, a very appealing, flourishing city. I decide I would love to return to these extraordinary mountain locations one day and learn more of the geography, explore the historical resonance and appreciate the grandeur in a more prepared and dignified state of mind.

I really had thought, like Sully all those years before, that I might perish in the mountains. His ancient predicament was different, yet it's the human terror so similar that I felt I was not alone in this ordeal. This kinship to the tramp's old terror brought a certain strange comfort. Now I know first-hand how he must have once felt.

7

Mudgee mysteries

Eventually I experience the rewards for surviving. My treat to myself is a fancy motel with en suite and TV. It costs more than double last evening's rate and there's no breakfast. I order a serve of freshly grilled fish and receive a double serve of chips. (I am their last customer of the evening.) All washed down with a bottle of cider. I purchase the seafood from a shop directly opposite the imposing Methodist, now Uniting, church. It's definitely the most imposing one I've seen. It's prominently placed just off the wide main street on a significant cross street. In the morning, I will find out more about this church and parsonage and seek out the tramp's shed home.

Tomorrow is Monday. I've only been travelling two days. Right now it

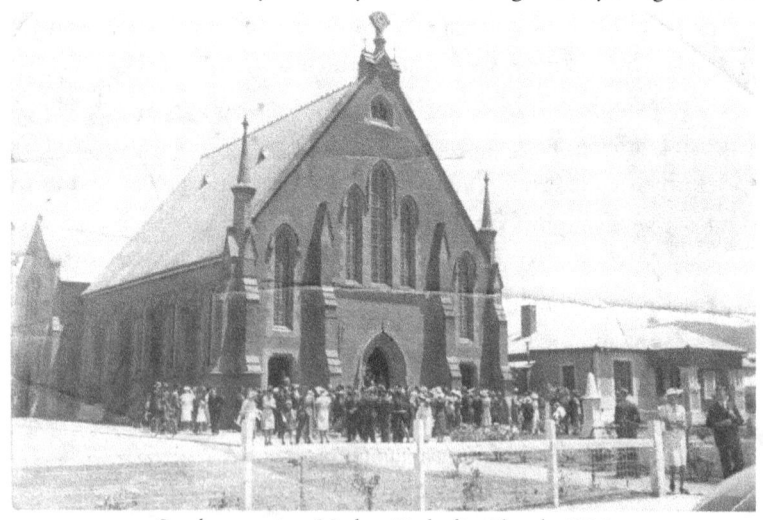

Sunday morning, Mudgee Methodist Church, 1930s

feels like two years. How much I have experienced and learnt. How many sites have I visited? Now they are all converging in my mind into one glorious post-stress muddle. The chronologies of the tramp and my father are becoming more confused than ever. I need to sit somewhere for a few days to try and sort it all out. Should I stay a second night in Mudgee? Right now, I can't bring my brain to decide on anything.

How wonderful sleep is when it finally comes. It restores confidence, capability and enthusiasm. The next morning, I am up early walking the waking streets of a surprisingly modern Mudgee, now the heart of a thriving wine industry and much more.

As I'd waited for my grilled fish with lemon the night before, I'd read the inscription on the church's memorial cairn to the Cornish Wesleyan minister, Thomas Angwin. The person who had caused this marvellous church to be built had died suddenly in 1865 aged thirty-five years. That was very strange. I could remember that my mother's father's name was Henry Thomas Angwin Shield. It could not be coincidence. But EMG had never mentioned this connection of hers to Mudgee. It's not until my return to Tasmania that I transcribe my mother's thirty-year-old tapes and learn more.

> My father's name was Henry Thomas Angwin Shield. He was called after a Methodist minister whom they thought very highly of. One of his brothers was Horatio something after another minister but I don't remember it all. There was Lionel Wesley and a sister who was Pearl; I don't think she had a second name. My father was the eldest. We knew his mother and father; they were Grandma and Grandpa to me. They stayed with us when we came down to live in Leichardt. Eventually they went to a Home, Grandpa died while we were at Leichardt and then Grandma after a while went to a home for elderly people.
>
> They were great old Methodists, Grandpa was a local preacher. They used to call him 'Holy Billy'. Shield was their name. He was William, I don't remember Grandma's name. We never used first names, but he was William. They were English, they'd come from England both of them and one of them was connected to Wales.
>
> Otherwise they were from the north of England. Dad's people were remotely connected with Captain Cook, from the same part of England too but a sideline. He never had any descendants so we are not descended from

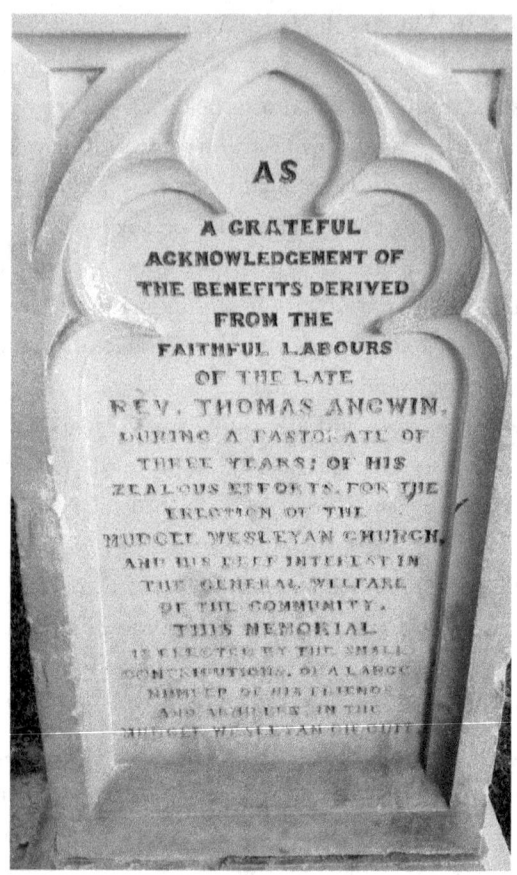

Memorial plaque, Mudgee

him but one of Cook's sisters was an aunt I think. But we never really worked that out. We are in that family descent. My father was born in Australia. We weren't interested in family backgrounds. I had cousins on my father's side but I've lost touch with them because we moved about so much and they were mostly in Sydney or round about.

My visit to Mudgee has unexpectedly brought into focus the third significant person in the story of the swagman and the parson – the parson's wife. One could almost say 'the elephant in the room'. Sorry, Mum, but I do so love elephants. EMG was always there, sustainer of the home and co-worker in the church. She always accepted Sully the swagman's residence in their back sheds.

Here I am in Mudgee, expecting to learn more of Sully's and my father's lives and staring me in the face is the answer to the strange middle names of my mother's father. Using my smartphone, I search for Thomas Angwin, a nineteenth-century Wesleyan Methodist evangelist from Cornwall.

The Maitland Mercury & Hunter River General Advertiser, Thursday 8 August 1867 (New South Wales)

MUDGEE (From the *Western Post*, August 2.)
  THE REV. THOMAS ANGWIN – It is our painful duty to chronicle in this issue the death of the above named gentleman, which took place at his residence in Church-street, yesterday afternoon. It is needless to say that the profound sympathy of all classes is expressed for his relatives under the affliction, and that not only by that particular body in which he had so long laboured as a devoted and faithful pastor, but by others, of various shades of religious opinion, who were simply identified with him socially. The deceased gentleman was a native of Cornwall, in England, and commenced his ministerial labours in this colony about 12 years ago. As the respective spheres of his duty, may be mentioned Singleton, Parramatta, Bathurst, Orange, the Goulburn district, and latterly Mudgee and Kiama. For three years he filled the office of minister here, and during that time, not only did he endear himself to his flock, but gained the lasting esteem of his fellow ministers of other denominations, as well as the respect of their people by his simplicity of character and his truly Christian demeanour.

He had died of tuberculosis leaving a wife, two children and a very large circle of friends to mourn their loss, as reported in *The Sydney Morning Herald*, Wednesday 7 August 1867.

Despite, or maybe because of, his imposing name, EMG's father had not led the shining Methodist life his parents hoped. Whereas RFG (his son-in-law) had made his own decision to ministry, Henry Thomas Angwin Shield had little interest in religion or the church. He worked in shops, at first in country towns. He'd met his Anglican wife in Orange. Later he was employed at Anthony Horderns huge store in Sydney. At one time he sailed with Burns Philp to Samoa to work as a shopkeeper/storeman. He was a drinker and would lose jobs easily. My mother said he drank even more in the Pacific. I'm hoping that's all he did.

Henry Thomas Angwin Shield, 1895

One of my elder sisters remembers him chasing Grandma Gibson, RFG's indomitable mother, around the parsonage asking for a kiss, or more. Did he still drink when he stayed with the family in Temora – possibly. With his rejection of his father 'Holy Billy's' fervour, he became a knockabout man of his day. The other side of the coin perhaps to Sully the earnest swagman. Mr Sully the non-drinker, born about the same time, had an opposite childhood as the son not of a wowser but of an alcoholic father.

Whatever my mother knew of this past connection to her father, she had clear and happy memories of her own time in Mudgee.

Methodist magazine, Mudgee

We had a different sort of older church... They built these shops and the parsonage was getting a bit small for anyone with much family. They ... built these three rooms across the front and you had to go through these three front rooms...[into] the house [at the]...back... [There] was the study and drawing room and a bedroom.

When a poor shivering chap came...asking about getting married, he had to come inside where the Ladies Church Aid were meeting in that

Uniting Church, Mudgee, 2015

middle room and go through to the study… The whole thing was a bit silly. But that's what they do sometimes with these things. We got around that and we loved it and we used to have a lot of church aid meetings in the house… We were always next door to the church. That was all right and it worked itself out.

In those days Comrades [a church club for teenage girls] were beginning to come in and we started Comrades in Mudgee. I'd had something to do with Comrades before… when we were in Leichardt I think. We had quite a good comradeship there and then another lady took over the Rays [for younger girls] and we had both of them. It was a very busy time. We used to have concerts. Even I used to get up and spout a few pieces of poetry by Banjo Patterson or someone if required. Not that I did much of that sort of thing but it was quite a busy time, there. We enjoyed it all; we liked it very much.

Before her marriage, EMG had her own experience working with teenage girls. She had established the first Cooma Girl Guide troop. Muriel had been appointed as a first year out English and history teacher to the brand new Cooma High School. The early 1920s saw the establishment of a range of country high schools throughout NSW. In a way, although she had to give up teaching on marriage and pay back her teaching bond, EMG did continue a professional life in her public role of minister's wife. All ministers were married men and it was, in one sense, a joint task, even if the team was billed as Rev. & Mrs R.F. Gibson.

First Cooma Girl Guides Troup, 1923; EMG centre 2nd row

Next door to Thomas Angwin's Wesleyan Methodist church is a new upmarket coffee nook. It's open for people on the way to work – a sure sign that sophisticated modern Australia has arrived. I wander around to the back of the church property on the next side street. There is an extensive age care facility. I imagine somewhere among it was once the shed, or was it a stone built coach house where Sully lived and prepared his puftalooners. It's all gone now. Even the add-on to the parsonage that had caused my mother some dismay is gone. In its place is some sort of shop.

What really entertains my bizarre sense of humour are the restricted parking signs in the driveway of the church. After eighty years, the church still has links to commerce in this town.

On the door of the newish hall adjoining the old imposing church is a sign advising needy callers to try the Catholics or Anglicans when (as now) it is closed.

Later, after checking out of the motel, I find there is still no one at the church or hall for me to talk to. Reluctantly, towards noon, I leave Mudgee via the Castlereagh Highway, confident that I will not be heading for the sort of unexpected surprise of yesterday. After filling up with fuel, I am amazed that my old Toyota Camry requires neither oil nor water. Good old 'Ashoka 3' has stood by me well.

8

Blucher boots

The historic hill town of Gulgong is only a short distance from Mudgee. Here in a sense I encounter Henry Lawson. Thanks to Wikipedia, I've already gained a fair idea of what the old blucher boots Sully used to wear looked like – strong lace-up, ankle boots. I'd also digressed to learn about the irascible old Prussian general himself. Possibly Blucher did more than the British under Wellington to defeat Napoleon at Waterloo. Wellington boots, almost knee-high and waterproof, taller than bluchers, are still well known today, bluchers less so.

To a Pair of Blucher Boots

Old acquaintance unforgotten,
Though you may be 'ugly brutes' –
Though your leather's cracked and rotten,
Worn-out pair of Blucher boots.
'Tis the richer man before you,
Dearer leathers grace his feel;
'Twas the better man that wore you
In the tramps through dust and heart!
Oft rebuffed by 'super's' snarling,
When I asked him for a 'show"
On that long tramp to the Darling
In the days of long ago;
Tell me, if you know it, whether,
As I sadly tramped away,

> Bore I heavy on your leather,
> Worn-out pair of Bluchers, say?
> Though your leather's cracked and rotten,
> Though you may be ugly brutes,
> I'll preserve you unforgotten,
> Worn-out pair of Blucher boots!
>
> Henry Lawson, 1890

Henry Lawson, like Sully, was an interesting product of rural NSW and Victoria. His eulogy to the blucher boot resonates with what must have been Sully's own sentiments. Nothing is more important than footwear when trudging (as Sully did in later life) or tramping, as he had when younger and the smell of the eucalypt and the road before him was fresh and new.

At Gulgong, I idle past an interesting old pub and a store. Tourists are arriving by car and bus. The narrow winding street becomes crowded. I pass an Indian restaurant, a newish one, but find myself wondering if the old Afghan cameleers and their teams ever passed this way.

Further along, the Henry Lawson museum is open. I spend thirty minutes sharing a cuppa and biscuit, chatting and browsing with the two women who are its volunteer guides today. Poor Henry, with his Norwegian father and activist Australian mother, had led a complicated and frequently alcoholic short life. He had a real bond with Mary Gilmore. Lawson (Larson) was a sensitive and sometimes tormented soul. I am sure many of his words express similar joys and trials to Sully's own life on the road.

From Gulgong, I take less travelled roads up through Coolah, where I put on my own Blundstone boots (not, I imagine, dissimilar to blucher boots) to walk across some mud and order from a roadside van at the crossroads a very insipid weak coffee.

Eventually I manoeuvre myself on to Gunnedah, which does not live up to my earlier memories of it. It's no place to stay the night, though it's getting on to evening. A big Angus at MacDonald's beside schoolchildren flirting on iPhones and I depart again, heading towards Armidale. From the Oxley Highway to the New England Highway, the largest NSW inland road, route 15.

The night deepens as I drive and oncoming headlights strain my eyes. One large vehicle after another passes. No sooner do I adjust back to high beam than I have to dip my lights again. The glare is disorienting but I keep on. There should be parking bays but I can't distinguish them in the darkness, with the glaring lights of oncoming transports.

Eventually I turn off the highway and find my way into the heart of Armidale. Too tired to look for accommodation, I put my seat back and fall asleep for a few hours, wrapped in blankets with my boots still on and a thick pair of socks. This is cold country.

From Armidale, I continue to Glen Innes, book a motel and spend the day exploring, recovering, eating and reading my notes. This is the last of my unplanned journeying. From now on, I'll have friends and family to visit and stay with. Life will be more straightforward.

Further on, I search both the Queensland and NSW side of the border (at Mudgeeraba and Murwillumbah) but am unable to locate an old photo of my father, RFG, mounted and dressed in his AIF Light Horse uniform. I can remember seeing it once. Perhaps my best bet now is to try and locate it on Trove, the wonderful repository of digitised newspapers.

The coastal journey from the Gold Coast south along the Pacific Highway and the enjoyable coastal detours to Fingal and Ballina pass without incident. I pull into the driveway of my sister-in-law's house in Newcastle. Barbara has lived here with my brother Ken (now sadly deceased) for over fifty years. Their four sons are all married with almost adult children of their own. They still remember their Papa (RFG), eating the brown bananas, and are inheritors of the Gibson surname, despite their many other lines of descent. (Barbara's parents came from Yorkshire.)

Newcastle, Mayfield to be specific, was the high point of RFG's career in the ministry. He recalled,

> There's no promotion in our church. They were all considered more or less equal. The best would be President of the Conference. I never collected

that. I was in charge of a district of about 60 ministers in Newcastle. I was chairman of several districts, it depends how many other ministers were in those districts.

But of course as Chairman you're more or less in charge of every circuit and the ministers. If a minister was in trouble or if he needed anything special, he had his own circuit stewards, the men that were in charge of running his circuit with him. As the Chairman of the District I was responsible for the whole district of about 30 circuits. And they'd come to me if there were problems. If they were moving and had been invited somewhere, they would come to ask if I could help them get the place they wanted.

I remember one year I had about 12 ministers to change. I got every one of them in the circuit they wanted but not myself. That was the year I was going out of Newcastle. I was invited to Hornsby but was sent to Hurlstone Park in Sydney. I was beaten but I got every other man in. You can do a lot as Chairman for a man. You could just stand up for him in the right place at the right time.

During the second of his five years in Mayfield, the *Newcastle Morning Herald* published the article about RFG reproduced on the following page.

Personality...

Rev. R. F. Gibson, Chairman of Newcastle district of the Methodist Church, claims to know New South Wales better than most people do.

He was born at Dapto in 1896, and entered Leigh Methodist College, Enfield, in 1919. He was one of the first ministers to take the United Faculty of the Methodist, Presbyterian and Congregational Churches at St. Andrew's College, Sydney University. He received his Diploma of Licentiate of Theology from Melbourne College of Divinity in 1922.

His first circuit was Cooma-Bombala, a wide area which he traversed on a motor-cycle. He travelled widely in New South Wales. During the war, as chairman of the Cootamundra district, he was chaplain to the R.A.A.F. training station at Temora. He came to Newcastle two years ago, and is in charge of Mayfield circuit.

9

An ending

Sully had died in Sydney before the family moved north to Newcastle (from Chatswood). Now RFG, his wife and youngest daughter (myself), moved back too, from Newcastle to Sydney.

Jen Gibson, Sydney, 1950s

When our father Russell Gibson died, my elder sister Raye wrote the following as part of a eulogy for him.

Administering at the Hurlstone Park circuit was a busy and happy time for Rev & Mrs Gibson and daughter Jen. The other children had married and were living elsewhere. As usual, there was a dog family member; an abundant vegetable garden and colourful flowers. Mrs Gibson had a flair for flower arrangements in the home and church.

Rev Gibson was concerned with healing and gave healing treatment in the form of laying on of hands with the officiating minister at Christ Church, St Lawrence in Sydney. He was emphatic that all healing and prayer for renewal was done in the name of Jesus Christ.

For one year Rev & Mrs Gibson and Jen transferred to Market Rasen in Lincolnshire, England. He was requested to stay for another year. In the

Jen Gibson, RFG and EMG, England, 1958

United Kingdom, he found that the concept of a minster as preacher-advisor was sought, and that the few old rigid teaching methods still evident there, were resented and on the way out.

Returning to Australia, Mr Gibson resumed his ministerial duties at the Malvern Hill circuit (Croydon, Sydney), taking heavy financial debts out of the red.

Rev & Mrs Gibson purchased their retirement home at Bundeena on the south coast of NSW. In their retirement years, many old and young church folk and friends visited there, some staying longer and living in a cabin on the block. Mr Gibson was always active. He took the Anzac Service for the Returned Services League each year, and prepared the way for the Bundeena Bowling Club to become a viable project. As well as a bowler, he was a competent and popular treasurer.

After retirement in 1966 Rev & Mrs Gibson drove to Western Australia to take the circuit of Hilton Park, Perth. There, he was interested in the different state and church regulations. For the first few nights, they slept on borrowed mattresses, as a minster in Western Australia supplies his own furniture. He noted that the WA conference had a regulation that no minster be asked to take more than eight school classes. He took the eight classes.

In retirement, he was able to pursue his interests in psychic phenomena and was the President of the Psychic research Society in Sydney. In this capacity he was interviewed on radio and took part in a television program and wrote for the science journal of the University of Sydney.

[In 1968 Rev & Mrs Gibson took their reliable Holden across Bass Strait and for three months ministered at the main church in Launceston. They drove all over Australia with this car and a small caravan.]

In 1979 Rev & Mrs Gibson sold the Bundeena home and bought a unit at the Uniting Church Retirement Village at Caves Beach [near Newcastle]. Although several strokes had impaired his physical activities, he continued gardening (the paw paw trees are still prolific) growing flowers, vegetables and herbs all together.

Rev Russell French Gibson L Th. Departed this life aged 87 years, at Mayfield on 11th November, 1983.

There are many lives enriched by his life's service, and wherever he lived, there are trees and flowers beautifying these places.

Postscript

It was February 1983. My father was to live another nine months – he would die on my birthday. On this day in February, we'd asked him, 'Dad, is there anything in your life that you would like to have done and haven't done?'

There was a moment's pause as the question sank in and was considered. A small sparrow (the only bird life in the vicinity of his Mayfield nursing home) pecked at a few crumbs. My father had saved them from his afternoon tea biscuit. As he reflected, he'd sprinkled them along the veranda railing. His old bush acquaintance had done a similar thing many times for his precious birds.

After considering carefully, RFG answered. 'Yes, There was an old tramp once. I knew him years ago. For some time he lived in our shed at Mudgee. His name was Sully and he always had a dog with him or a pup. I would like to have recorded his story.'

'But Dad, you did. Don't you remember? You *have* written his story.'

RFG had forgotten. Now this small precious memory – a tiny cameo in Australia's heritage – is restored.

Sully's clerical family, c. 1941

Appendix

R.F. Gibson's Methodist Church circuits

Date	Place	Approx. time
1922	Bulli, NSW	3 months
1922–23	Cooma/Bombala, NSW	2 years
1923–24	Berrigan, Finlay, Tocumwal, NSW	1 year
1925–28	Boorowa (first married), NSW	3 years
1929–32	Austenham Road, Leichardt, NSW	3 years
1932–35	Coolamon, NSW	5 years
1935–39	Mudgee, NSW	5 years
1940–44	Temora, NSW	5 years
1945–47	Chatswood South, NSW	3 years
1948–52	Mayfield, Newcastle, NSW	5 years
1952–57	Hurlstone Park, NSW	5 years
1957–59	Lincolnshire, England, NSW	1 year
1960–65	'Malvern Hill', Croydon, NSW	5 years

After retirement

| 1966 | Hilton Park, WA | 1 year |
| 1968 | Launceston, Tasmania | 3 months |

Acknowledgements

I express my appreciation and thanks to Annaxue Yang, Julia Hammond, Robyn Mathison, Joan Broad and Lynne Dow, all of whom read the manuscript at various stages and offered many helpful suggestions and amendments. A thank you to my sister Raye for additional photographs; and to the many relatives, relatives by marriage (especially my sister-law Barbara Gibson) and friends who showed interest and support.

Sully the Swagman apparently had no human descendants. However, there are possibly generations of country dogs (and a few less wild rabbits), descended from his beloved animal companions.

The following is a list of direct descendants of Russell and Muriel Gibson as at 2016.

Beryl (Gibson) Midgley:
    Carol Meyer – Steven and Amira
    Robyn Bolton – Jamie and Andy Gawler (New Zealand)
    Christine (Tina) Boyd – Matt, Aleisha (+ Aria b. 2016) and Dylan

Raye (MacLeman) Gibson:
    Gar MacLeman
    Les MacLeman – Adelaide and Cameron MacLeman

Ken Gibson (and Barbara, née Lyon):
    Ross Gibson – Elizabeth and Harry
    Laurie Gibson – Kalinda, Perry, Beau and Ricky
    Jeff Gibson – Sophie, Nick and Josh
    Tone Gibson – Aidan and Grace

Jen Gibson:
    Nicolette Vaszolyi – Elliott Rider and Isabel Rider

This book is for Elliott Russell and Isabel Rose, my own grandchildren; for all the grandchildren and great-grandchildren of Russ and Muriel Gibson (included above); and for those still to come. It's for all with an interest in another small piece in the story of Australia and its unfolding sixty-thousand-year-old human tale; another piece in the expanding mosaic of our global human chronicle.

I express my gratitude to the heart-shaped jewel of the south, Tasmania, which has nurtured me for a decade now.

Jen Gibson
Helms Cottage, Tasmania
11 November 2016

www.ingramcontent.com/pod-product-compliance
Lightning Source LLC
Chambersburg PA
CBHW070910080526
44589CB00013B/1245